# A
# WANNABE
# COWBOY

**Before Alaska: Horse and
wagon use on a
Montana ranch in the 1950s**

Jake Jacobson
Alaska's Favorite Real Life Wilderness Storyteller

PUBLICATION
CONSULTANTS
WE BELIEVE IN THE POWER OF AUTHORS

PO Box 221974 Anchorage, Alaska 99522-1974
books@publicationconsultants.com, www.publicationconsultants.com

ISBN Number: 978-1-63747-314-6
eBook ISBN Number: 978-1-63747-315-3

Library of Congress Number: 2023914340

Manufactured in the United States of America

# A WANNABE COWBOY

My earliest childhood recollections are of barnyard animals such as our hogs, milk cows, horses, chickens, cats, dogs, and ducks, along with pestiferous pigeons and ubiquitous rats that required our attention to eliminate. I loved them all - except the rats. A very lucky kid, I was - to be in the company of so many animals - and I always felt like I was most fortunate!

Early on I decided that I wanted to be a cowboy, not like the gunslingers or stagecoach robbers, but a garden-variety cowpuncher, engaging in roping, throwing, branding, and all the usual stuff. The fancy, fringed clothes of Roy Rogers and Gene Autry turned me off. I preferred the garb of everyday, working cowboys, like the ones I saw on the TV programs Rawhide and *Gunsmoke* -and like the clothes worn by real cowmen that we knew - like our own normal everyday work or play clothes.

My Dad (Pop) often took me hunting and fishing with him. So did Grandpa Jacobson and some of my uncles. One of my aunts took me fishing often. Together we pursued wild ducks, pheasants, and rabbits, primarily. When the demands of the pursuit required, Pop would pick me up, either stuff me into his backpack or tell me to hang onto his neck, and off we would go, chasing down a grounded duck or pheasant. Before I entered grade school, Pop had taken me on a couple of deer hunts. Those were my favorites. Dad used an old double-barreled Knickerbocker twelve-gauge shotgun with buckshot initially, then he began using a Mauser 8mm bolt action rifle with a swastika stamped on the barrel, that he had brought back from the war. He came home late one night from a deer hunt, covered with blood. I panicked when I saw him, thinking he had been shot, but he noticed my expression of terror and burst into laughter, which brought me to a similar state, but I was confused until I saw the big mule deer buck he had wrangled into the trunk of the car.

My childhood memories include Pop taking off his clothes - all but his shorts - to enter the muddy Rio Grande River and grope along under the steep banks for catfish. Those big channel cats scared me a little, but I studied their dorsal and pectoral fins and barbs and figured I could avoid painful injury by being careful about how I grabbed the fish. Securing such an impressive, tasty trophy was clearly worth some risk. That's called noodling now, but we just called it hand fishing. I learned how to carefully grab a catfish by the lower jaw and hold the writhing body away to avoid getting stuck by a barb or a fin. I knew that a good meal is worth some risk.

The special thrill of taking a game animal is as hard for me to describe now as it was more than seventy years ago. The death of any animal is sad, but the success of the pursuit is exhilarating beyond my ability to describe. On taking an animal, I've always had a smorgasbord of emotional rushes, from remorse at the death of the beautiful animal, and the coming loneliness of its mates, to thoughts of the delicious meals it would provide. Sometimes there were trophies to be tacked to the wall and feelings of strength and purpose in the provision of food for the family. Of course, the trophy value is far surpassed by the nutritional worth, but that is not always clear in the mind of the hunter at the moment of the kill. Most thoughtful hunters struggle a bit with this I suspect - as I have. It is a unique experience - harvesting an animal for personal use. Several times I have witnessed hunters shed tears when they approach their lifeless quarry. I have shed some tears myself on some such occasions, but I always tried to keep others from seeing me weep. There are mysteries in life and in the nature of man. I still ponder this and other unquantifiable aspects of life and human nature.

So early on, I realized that I have far more questions than answers for the imponderables of life.

Our domestic stock occupied a special place in my heart. These animals were primarily dependent on us for food as well as protection from weather, predators, and disease. A special responsibility - stewardship - goes along with having domesticated animals and pets. I suppose it is a feeling of inter-species paternalism that drives a pastoralist - or a kid doing his chores - to rise before dawn, gather the cows or goats for milking, inspect, tend their injuries, raise or purchase and preserve their winter fodder and protect them from predators. Our animals were on my mind almost all of the time. And to no less a degree of a concern than I had for the more charismatic big critters, feeding the chickens, and gathering their eggs gave me a sense of duty fulfilled, accompanied by profound contentment. Lucky are the children that grow up with stock to tend. Though I felt a special pain when it came time to kill a domestic animal to eat, I did it dutifully, quickly, and mercifully, and realized that one should avoid getting too emotionally attached to a stock animal. We avoided eye contact with the critter to be sacrificed. We did not name the animals we expected to eventually kill to eat.

My Dad was a miner and we lived in some pretty rough boom towns in the early 1950s. Grants, New Mexico was a desolate, nasty community with well-established gangs of Mexicans and Indians that were accustomed to picking on Anglos - or gringos, as they called us Caucasian kids. I recognized that one had to either battle their way to peer group respectability or submit to bullying by gang members. I chose to fight. Unrelated to my fighting we wound up moving more frequently than I liked.

By 1955 we had moved to a new copper mining site in southern Arizona. Unlike some of the other isolated, remote diggings, this big new development included a new town with a shopping center, hospital, and paved streets - all owned by the company. This was not my idea of a good place to live - it had too much cookie-cutter sameness. I preferred the little remote mining sites with their random groups of amateur-built homes, that didn't have a retail store or even a post office. In those rural settlements, we were able to keep a few domestic animals and a garden, both of which were important to me. But in the new company town, gardens, and livestock were not possible. It was way too civilized for me! So I worked at convincing myself that I could be content with whatever situation I was thrust into. I'd try to make the most of it. I focused on hunting rabbits, quail, and doves. Gardens were not thought possible in the sunbaked caliche soil of the desert. But that cactus-ridden desert had a surprising abundance of cottontail rabbits, Gamble quail, and other critters to pursue.

One of my eighth-grade teachers, Don "Catfish" McClure took a liking to me and took me along to catch snakes, kangaroo rats, and other critters to sell to the wildlife buyers in Tucson. He even paid me for helping! He took me hunting with a shotgun and rifle, too.

## A BAD HEART

I was blessed with wonderful parents, and I always wanted to please them. I wanted them to be proud of me. I wanted to be like them and most of the other members of our family.

My Dad had played basketball in high school, and I wanted to be like him in that way as well as others. I began playing with the high school team in our little town when I was in eighth grade. I had dreams of great athletic success. But when I went in for a physical in my freshman year, a young, newly arrived mining company doctor, with a horrible bedside manner, detected a heart murmur with his stethoscope. First, he made a remark about my red pubic hair, which profoundly embarrassed me. When he put a stethoscope to my chest, he noticed my mild heart murmur and overreacted, asking me in front of the other kids, if I'd ever had "Saint Vitus Dance" - which I had read about in the Huckleberry Finn book and I knew that those so afflicted showed involuntary spastic jerks and twitches. In that little town in 1956, being called "spastic" was as grave an insult as being called a queer. I hoped the other guys didn't know the significance of Saint Vitus Dance! (But most didn't read that much, anyway.) That same day the doctor put me on monthly injections of Bicillin and ordered me to not be physically active, as he believed I had a case of Rheumatic Fever, which was the cause of my murmur. Worst of all, his remarks were heard by all my schoolmates that were in the exam room. So I was marked as a physically defective boy. That was hard for me to swallow. I was devastated … and profoundly angry. I felt abused and robbed!

As I walked home in the choking sulfur smoke from the smelter, I decided that if my ticker was weak, I would try to find out right away, and if it was bad, I'd sure as heck not waste any more time in school than was absolutely necessary. If it looked like I was not going to live long, I planned to spend my limited number of days joyfully hunting, fishing, and embracing nature with my dog, Gyp. I would live outdoors, full-time. I might even become a hermit.

Then after the bad news began to soak in, I got really angry with that inexperienced, arrogant young doctor. But birds of a feather and people of the same profession stick together to protect members of their group - their brethren. After my folks took me to discuss my situation with the older, head company doctor, he did not offer any special tests, nor did he counter the diagnosis and prescription of the younger medical man. I still believe he did that to avoid wounding the ego of the young physician. Both were salaried employees of the big mining company and those physicians stuck up for each other. The health services were provided to employees at a low cost and that was that. Few people knew enough or had enough money to demand second opinions, let alone an examination by a specialist. Like most people, my parents naively assumed that everything that was done by "our" doctors was in our best interest, as all doctors surely followed their Hippocratic Oath, so we would just have to learn to deal with my situation, and I would have to learn to live with it. No one challenged the egocentric young doctor's hasty, and what proved to be, an erroneous diagnosis, regarding my heart. Questioning it never crossed our minds. We naively trusted the big mining company and its doctors.

I felt like I was being smothered by the restriction of not being allowed to participate in basketball. My dreams of adventure were canceled. But as much as I liked books, I resolved that I would not become just a bookworm!

After a week or so of dark and dismal depression - none of us knew the term depression related to anything but economic hard times back then - I started running to and from school. I made up dumbbells and barbells out of coffee cans and buckets filled with concrete, connected by a piece of pipe. I stretched old rubber bicycle inner tubes from our porch posts and exercised every part of my body that I could think of. I was going to test how weak or strong my ticker and the rest of my body parts really were. I aimed to find out if I was fit or not, - and I became stronger and more fit in the process.

My poor mother was distraught at my lack of compliance with the doctor's orders to take it easy, but Pop told her that worrying would do no good as I was as strong-willed and stubborn as she and others in our family, so Pop convinced Mom that it was best they allow their hard-headed son to do his thing.

Mom died way too young, and I have always thanked her and God that she did not show her worries about my physical efforts any more than she did. No one ever had better parents and family than those with which I had been blessed, and the results of their parentage have been among the greatest gifts - blessings is a more accurate description - I have ever been given. The ovarian/sperm lottery had been kind to me and others in our family for generations.

With the runs to school and other exercises, I grew stronger and developed nearly unlimited stamina. I just would not quit - and I felt good. The best overall athletes in my class were no doubt stronger and some could outlast me - maybe, but we never had an opportunity to compete.

But other boys of my age teased me mercilessly in school about not engaging in sports. Some, but only a few, were ornery about it. Some suggested that I was chicken. They did not know that I had decided that as I had nothing to lose, I would fear nothing at all. I would not tolerate anyone thinking I was afraid of anything, so when teased abusively, I would fly into the face of my tormentor, and as a result, I got into a lot of fistfights. I lost about as many fisticuffs as I won, but anyone dealing with me knew they would have a real fight on their hands and I would do my best to win. Years before, in Grants, New Mexico, I had made up my mind that no one would ever hurt me in a fistfight, no matter where or how hard I was hit. I believed that ... and it worked. I stifled and denied both pain and fear. At the end of my sophomore year in High School, I was kicked out of school for fighting too much, after I damaged a popular athlete.

I didn't care at all about being expelled. It meant more time for me to pursue rabbits and quail, whether in season or out. Besides, if my heart was bad, I had nothing to lose. At age sixteen, I decided to become a professional hunter, beginning by focusing on cottontail rabbits.

One evening shortly after I had been expelled, I came home with a couple of cottontail rabbits and some out-of-season Gamble quail. Mom and Pop asked me to skin and dress the animals on the porch and then sit down at the kitchen table. Pop said they had some very good news for me. Mom was nearly in tears. But I could see they were happy tears.

Immediately I envisioned a job on a tuna fishing boat. I had seen movies of men with long poles hoisting huge tuna up over the rails and onto the deck. Or, I thought just maybe, it would be a job as a cowboy with my Uncle Stan in Montana. I was nearly breathless as I yanked the skins off of the rabbits and birds.

Mom told me that her brother, my Uncle Stan, had offered me a full-time job on the ranch in Montana for which he was foreman. I had to bite my lip to hold back the tears! I'd been asking God every day for a sign, for relief - just anything to show that he heard my prayers.

In bed that night I thanked God for his wondrous benevolence. This was going to be even better than being on a tuna boat!

Mom added that the school would allow me to re-enter the coming fall, so long as I avoided so many pugilistic encounters. The high school counselor knew of my situation, and he had interviewed some of the fellows I had mixed it up with and most of them admitted to maliciously taunting me. My grades had always been top-notch, even with my usual minimal effort at homework, and that, no doubt, would help the counselor get me back into high school. The counselor reported that he believed that I had "promise" - that I might even amount to something, someday. In 2015 I attended a High School reunion and offered copies of my first two books as a door prize. The classmate who won them asked me to sign them and then mentioned, in front of his wife and other schoolmates, that I had beaten the tar out of him when we were sophomores. I told him that I honestly didn't recall, but I asked him what the issue had been. He said that he was being a jerk teasing me about my weak heart and that he deserved the whipping I gave him. That was a fight that I didn't even recall. It must not have been a difficult encounter. I admired the courage it took for him to tell me that story.

Mom wanted my word that I would try to use good sense with my heart situation, to be sure to get the double Bicillin shots (one initially painful injection in each buttock every month - but after a few months of injections, they no longer hurt) and come home in time for school in September, at least until I graduated from high school.

Without much discussion or hesitation, I agreed to Mom's terms. I would have agreed to anything to get to Montana!

## Deliverance to Montana, And A Surprise "Welcome"

It was my first trip on a commercial airline. A shiny silver DC3 took me from Tucson to Denver, Colorado. After a short stop, we stopped in Caspar, Wyoming, crossed the Yellowstone River which brought to my mind many historical memories, and then we landed at Great Falls, Montana. Stan met me at the airport, we shook hands, retrieved my single checked bag, and walked to the parking lot. Not a lot was said, but Uncle Stan was never long on words. Stan opened the trunk of his little Ford and put my suitcase in the back. As he closed the lid he said he understood that I seemed to like to fight and he landed a solid right in the middle of my chest. I was on the ground, stunned. Stan told me that if I got the urge to fight, I should try him first. He added that fighting was not allowed on the ranch. I was in shock, but I got myself up without saying a word and climbed into the passenger seat of the Ford. There was no need for understanding, empathy, or any of that pseudo-psychological stuff. This was tough love, for sure. The law was simply, clearly, laid down. There was work to be done and nothing was to interfere with the work - especially not fighting. This was not the reception I had expected.

Great Falls Airport terminal in late May 1958.

Stan drove downtown to a general store that was stocked with lots of cowboy work gear and picked out some Tony Lama cowboy boots that cost twenty-two dollars. I balked. I didn't want such expensive boots, and I never cared for pointy-toed cowboy boots, anyway, but Stan insisted and said I could pay him back later. I never did like those durned boots. Then I got a pair of Red Wing knockoffs that cost six bucks - more to my liking and those I would wear every day that I wasn't on a horse using the pair of old spurs that Stan gave me. A wide-brimmed, cowboy-style straw hat completed my outfit, and we were off to get hamburgers and head to the ranch. Stan never talked much, but he did say we had a lot of work to catch up on after he had taken the day off to retrieve me from the airport.

He added that he expected me to not let him down.

I asked where we were headed and was told that we'd spend most of our time in the Little Belt Mountains, south of Cascade. The headquarters site was right on the bank of Little Hound Creek. Three other ranch properties made up the Staunton Ranch Company. The Loy Place sat next to the Missouri River near the small town of Cascade, the Whitmore Place was located in the foothills. The headquarters on Little Hound Creek was 20 miles Southwest of the Whitmore Place and the summer range, Elk Horn, was forty miles further back into the mountains.

Stan showed me a little one-room log cabin next to his cabin where I would stay. But I was to share it with a misfit kid who, at nineteen, was three years older than me, about four inches taller, and outweighed me by forty pounds. That was a lot of difference in weight and age. I was sixteen, skinny, and still a kid. He looked more like an onery man than a boy. The cook was his grandmother.

This guy, Eddie was a real jerk and a wannabe bully. I overheard one of the men say that Eddie had recently done some time in a Montana reform school and his grandma was trying to straighten him out. His manners at the cook house were fine, as everyone knew that Stan and the manager, John Hannibal "Peck" Wareheim would tolerate no rudeness, swearing, or other discourteous behavior from anyone, especially in the presence of women. Stan and Peck were not weekly churchgoers, but they were strict, and never irreverent. But once Eddie thought no one was looking or listening, his monster side appeared and dominated him. You might say he let his badger loose easily.

After a big, tasty dinner, including fresh apple pie, Stan and I went to the shop to replace some broken rack poles on the bull rake that Eddie had been driving. I wasn't much help, but I was paying attention and learning. I figured Eddie must be with his Grandma, being counseled by her, maybe even washing dishes. Stan and I worked until we finished, well after dark.

When I got to my cabin, Eddie was ready, and primed to exert his dominance. He pushed me roughly up against the door and told me that he was the boss of the cabin and I had better never forget it.

This had been a uniquely interesting, but exasperating day, and I was pretty much at my wit's end, so I just listened to bully Eddie tell me what a tough guy he was and went to bed, exhausted.

But I knew that very soon I was going to have to fight ... and beat ... this ornery bully. He was probably the most despicable of all self-made bastards that I had thus far encountered in life.

Thankfully I lapsed into somnolent oblivion until Stan's loud knocking on the door announced it was time to go to breakfast. It wasn't even daylight yet.

My wife, Teresa, daughter Kate and me at "my log cabin" in
2008 - more than fifty years later.

Plenty of pancakes, fried eggs, bacon, butter, toast, and jam were on the table and everyone was stuffing themselves to the point of distention and discomfort, so I followed suit. I had never eaten such a huge breakfast in my life, up to that point. But in that era, before anyone dreamed up coffee breaks, there would be no snacks or pauses, only the water jug, and a few brief pee stops until lunchtime, so I was getting fortified. I was close to throwing up when I staggered out of the cook shack, but I managed to keep it all down. That became my breakfast routine on the ranch.

We went to the corral and Stan picked two medium-sized work-horses, Boots, a mare, and Freddie, the gelding. He showed me how to harness the horses - I was trying to remember all the harness terms - collar, hames, quarter straps, breeching straps, tugs, back strap, belly strap, reins - it was a lot of new stuff and terms. And I was fully engaged in this interesting new activity.

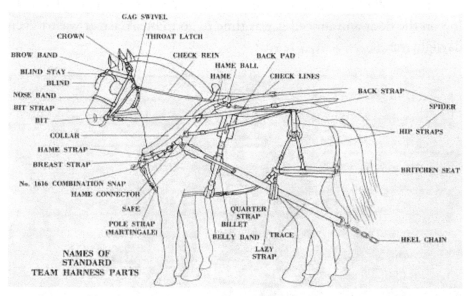

A diagram like the one above would have helped me memorize the terms.

Once the horses were harnessed, we hitched them up to the buck-board. Stan cautioned me to always hook up the tugs (traces, in movie lingo) to the single trees just before getting on the rig and to always discon-nect them before leaving the rig for any reason - whatsoever. This was to prevent a runaway team from carrying off whatever the team was hitched to. With the tugs disconnected, should they take off, the team would run with only the neck yoke, not dragging the rig behind, spooking them and leading to damage to the rig itself and maybe resulting in injury to the horses, and people. We walked the team to one of the buckboards and hooked up.

One of the buckboard wagons with a team ready to go to the hayfield.

Stan told me to get up on the seat and drive the wagon up the hill to the big hay field. A heavy work team, Chub, and Sally followed us on a lead rope. Stan gave me a constant stream of advice and pointers during the mile-and-a-half trip, including advice that I could ride the mare, Boots, as a saddle horse, but Freddie was too twitchy for that. I was to talk gently to the horses and never use the reins to slap their backs to get them to go faster - that's just movie stuff, he told me. That and a lot of other stuff one sees in movies is not a good technique in the real work of driving teams of horses or mules.

When we stopped at the partially completed loose stack Stan hooked the bigger team up to the overshot stacker. Then he showed me how to unhook my rake team and move them to the dump rake. He said he was sure I would pick up on what to do pretty quickly and cautioned me to watch out for buzztails or rattlesnakes, as most people called them. If one came up pierced by a rake tooth, it should be carefully removed.

Stan gripped one of the rake tines and ran his hand from the spring a the base to the tip, which was honed sharp from being dragged along the ground.

"Sharp as a dueling sword, make sure you don't wind up with one or more piercing you, always be careful and watch for things that can cause you grief or injury," he said.

Pete and Milly pulling me on the dump rake - with tines like rapiers.

By the time I was ready to begin wind rowing the hay that had been cut the day before, two other tractor-powered rigs were out making the rounds cutting with seven-foot mower blades and Eddie was on the way with the motorized bull rake to the stacker's head with a load of hay. Two older men were on the loose stack with pitchforks, arranging each new load of hay to hold the stack together. The operation was fully in motion with lots of working men, horses, and other moving parts.

A motorized bull rake with turning wheels in the back allowed for sharp turns, but driving it took a little getting used to.

Delivering a bull rake load of hay to the overshot stacker head.

Up she goes. The load could be dumped long or short, depending on how
fast the stacker team pulled it.

17

A horse-powered overshot stacker at work. The stacker team was out of the picture to the far right. The load could be delivered to the far end of the stack by moving the horses faster, as shown here, or it could be dropped at the near end by walking slower.

This wasn't exactly what I had thought cowboying would be all about, but I was loving the whole scene, especially driving those well-trained horses. The ranch needed to put up hay feed to hundreds of cattle during the long, cold Montana winter and haying was the most demanding project of every summer.

We broke for lunch and went back to the cook house to once again overstuff our bellies. Everything tasted delicious in my ravenous state and my gut capacity was expanding. I was amazed at how much I could get down my neck and hold down. The old lady cook was worth her keep, even if it meant putting up with her miserable grandson.

About mid-afternoon, Eddie, through his usual arrogance and carelessness, had another wreck with the motorized bull rake. This time several of the rake head "teeth" (homemade from lodgepole pine) were busted and would have to be replaced. Stan went over to temporize the machine for transport to the shop that night. Eddie got sent to the headquarters to see what chores they could devise for him. Peck assigned him to clean out one section of the barn which had several months of accumulation of horse droppings that had become thoroughly infested with maggots. It was not a pleasant chore, especially once the top layer was removed which exposed the disgusting writhing white maggots and released some uniquely obnoxious odors. I was surprised to see how many maggots were slowly writhing in the rotten and smelly horse poop.

Eddie's hot rodding had damaged the bull rake two days in a row and Peck was not happy. A couple of prime-time hours - for six men - had been lost each day. Peck told Stan maybe he better run the rake the next day and Eddie would continue to shovel horse poop, which might be good for his brain and attitude. And as soon as could be, Peck said he wanted me trained to run the motorized bull rake.

Me bringing in a big load with the motorized bull rake.

With what little experience I had, I really liked driving the two medium-sized, fast, rake teams, which were alternated from one day to the next and I got that job most of the time, but I was resigned to doing whatever chore I was given. I owed a lot to Stan, Peck, and even Eddie, in his own special way, (which was due to his incompetence and nasty temper), and I was not going to renege on any of my obligations or job assignments to any of those people. But I figured I owed Eddie a serious whooping.

With the steering wheels in the back, the bull rake took some getting accustomed to, but was far more maneuverable than a machine with front-wheel steering. It responded quickly to the slightest change in direction and after an hour or so I really liked driving it, but, still, I much preferred using the horses.

The machine had a hand crank to lower the rake head teeth for gathering up bunches of loose hay off the ground. Then the head was raised for the high-speed trip back to the stacker. When delivered to the stacker's head, the bull rake head was dropped on the stacker's head to leave the hay, and the rig was backed off. When clear of the tines of the stacker's head, the bull rake head was cranked up and another fast run for more hay was made.

Somehow Eddie heard of the plans to put me in his place on the bull rake and that really soured him. That evening as I took the harnesses off and grained my team, while no one was looking, Eddie deliberately tossed a fork load of stinking, maggot-saturated horse poop at me, but he missed. I knew our time was coming. I was going to wait for a good opportunity to bust that self-made S.O.B. I knew I could beat him - and I had to.

As I mentioned earlier, I'd made up my mind several years before that no one would hurt me in a fight - I just refused to feel any pain and that relieved me of fear, but not of the black eyes and cuts I received, - or my common sense.

Again, after supper, Stan and I replaced the several broken lodge pole pine rake teeth while Eddie continued to shovel horse manure from the barn stalls. Peck made sure he stayed on the job until well after dark this time.

I was in my bunk and asleep when Eddie banged his way into the cabin. I did not stir, but I half expected him to attack me, he was so badly twisted and angry, but he just took a swig from his secret little bottle of whiskey and crawled into his bunk. I thought he was acting like a petulant, spoiled little girl, but this wasn't the time to say it.

## DEALING WITH A DEVIL

The next morning it was raining and blowing too hard to do any haying, so Peck told Eddie and me to saddle up and move some cull heifers from one field to the next, and he said to be sure to get them all. He said it was no use to take the dog, a border collie named Pooch, as old Pooch would ignore anybody but Stan, so we went off in search of the cows without a dog, which neither of us had any experience using on cows anyway. We had sack lunches and water jugs for the day. Stan had given me a dandy pair of used batwing chaps, spurs, and an old leather jacket that made for really good, protective gear for riding through the chokecherry and thistle patches.

One of "my" favorite saddle horses, was this bay mare named Babe.

That day was most unpleasant in the driving, chilly rain, with Eddie shouting and cursing at me constantly. I figured I might just get in close and knock him off his horse, but he was so much bigger, I doubted my attempt would be successful and I might wind up on the ground, myself. I sure didn't want to botch this attempt. I decided I would have to wait for a better opportunity to settle with this ornery life-form, but I was rapidly nearing the limit of my personal tolerance.

We got all the heifers we could find - the count was right - gathered and moved to another pasture and headed back to the corral just before supper. Eddie was cussing and carrying on as usual about the rain and everything and everybody, especially me, but I didn't engage him verbally. I figured it best to not talk to him at all when he was throwing one of his fits.

With nobody apparently around to hear or see it, Eddie hollered at me ("you little Bastard") to open the gate, so I got off my horse and opened it. As Eddie passed through the gate, he spurred his horse and tried to run me down. But I was expecting trouble and I dodged in time.

However, Eddie was completely unprepared for what was coming next.

Grabbing his right forearm and coat tail as he came by, using all the strength and determination I had, I jumped off the ground to add my weight to the action. Eddie was completely taken by surprise. I jerked him clear off his horse. As he hit the mud his face was showing a mix of anger and surprise. I reckon he must have been in shock. I gave him my hardest kick in the ribs, then another and another, on the same side. I heard the air whooshing out of him on the last two kicks. Like most bullies, this guy was hollow and he folded when he was seriously threatened.

Then I stood over him and told him if he got up I would knock his ugly head clear off. (Actually, he wasn't bad looking, but he was sure ugly in nature.) He was hurting and just lay there looking angry at me. So I gave him another heavy kick on the other side and told him to wipe that mean look off his face. He seemed unconvinced, so I stomped him on the chest as hard as I could with the heel of my boot. I envisioned stomping him clear under the mix of mud and cow poop. He didn't want anymore and I stifled my urge to deliver more blows to my beaten, despised antagonist. At least for the moment, Eddie had given up - it's just like a bully to do that!

I figured those expensive, sharp-toed, and heeled cowboy boots might have earned part of their cost. It ran through my mind that I could give him a back kick with my spurs, but he had enough - and I figured I might lose my footing in the slick mix of mud and cow poop, so I quit where I was ... well ahead, for the moment.

I was so angry I had to fight back the tears, but I clenched my teeth and told him if he ever fooled with me again, I was going to hurt him really bad next time. He didn't say a word, or I would have smacked or stomped him again.

Leaving Eddie in the mud and rain, clutching his ribs, with his horse standing head down near the gate, I led my horse into the barn to take off my borrowed saddle, then wipe down and grain the horse.

As I approached the barn door, I noticed that Stan was standing just inside, out of the rain, smoking his usual cigarette. He made eye contact with me and just nodded his head once, approvingly, then without a word, he turned and walked to the cook shack. He had seen the whole incident and seemed to be good with it all.

And I felt good about it, too.

There were pitchforks and manure forks aplenty around the stalls. I knew that Eddie - mortified, and angry beyond description, would probably like to bury one in my guts, and he was twisted enough to do it, so as I rubbed down my horse and cleaned the mud from his legs and around the frogs of his hooves, I kept watching over my shoulder, but Eddie stayed outside in the corral with his horse still standing with its head down nearby, in the rain, until I left the barn. When he did walk in, he wasn't standing up real straight. He was kind of bent over to the left. He had some sore, maybe even busted, ribs, I reckoned, and that gave me a profound sense of satisfaction.

## A PASSAGE

As I walked in the drizzle toward the cabin, I felt strangely different. It was somehow similar to the feeling I had as I walked home in the choking sulfur smoke after being told that I had a bad heart and couldn't play basketball or be physically active. That was a dark, foreboding feeling, but the sensation this day was just the opposite - it was wonderful! I reckoned that I had made some sort of passage. I felt free and extra light on my feet. And, I smelled the wet grass. I was smelling Montana and I must have imprinted it, as whenever I return in early summer, I recognized that wonderful mix of odors and I experienced very deep, profound, and private joy.

## FEELING LUCKY .... AND FREE!

That was only the third time in my life that I had initiated a serious battle without giving the other guy any warning. Each time, my opponent was older, bigger, and appeared considerably tougher than me, so, figuring I needed all the help I could get, I took full advantage of the surprise ... and won two of those critical battles. I was certain that I would have to beat Eddie again in a fight for which he would give me no notice, as that had happened to me before with other bullies like him. I resolved to be ever-alert for his next big move.

I guess Stan and Peck thought twisted Eddie might attack me in my sleep, so they had him stay on the floor in his Grandma's room in the cook house that night. I didn't miss his company. To my surprise and joy, when breakfast was done, Peck told Eddie to gather up his stuff and put his gear in the back of the jeep as he was going to town.

Eddie was canned! I never saw him again, but I heard that he wound up in the county jail not long thereafter. That figured.

I was now free of one of the most disgusting bullies I had ever encountered and I also had the little log cabin all to myself, at least until they could find another haying hand! And I felt ever so lucky. No ... more than that, I felt truly blessed. I thanked God in the newfound privacy of my cabin.

Stan and Peck were never long on compliments, but old Peck -his real name was John Hannibal Wareheim - would chuckle a little every now and then with a wry comment that in a roundabout way, sort of let me know he approved of my performance with Eddie. Out of deference to the old cook, Peck had agreed to hire Eddie in the hope that honest work might straighten him out, and he was no doubt relieved to no longer have that burdensome, and potentially dangerous guy on the place.

Haying was going well and it looked like we might get a third cutting, but we were a few men short of what Peck figured was needed, so since I was due to go to Great Falls for my monthly double Bicillin shots, Peck told me I should drive him to town that day in the big International Harvester cattle truck because we had some men and supplies to pick up down on skid row after my visit to the Doctor's office. The nurse gave me the two jabs and I left.

I always liked driving big trucks, especially the big International with its extra gearing, so this looked like it was going to be an especially interesting day for me.

The Staunton Ranch Company's International stock truck.

## ASSISTING IN THE SHANGHAI

After my monthly pain in the butt Bicillin shots (which long before I had convinced myself were just inconvenient, more than painful) we loaded some feed, mineral salt, and other materials, then went down to skid row. "The Mint" bar was full of drunks and the street out front had several inebriated bums hanging around. I could smell their stale, cigarette, and alcohol-tainted breath along with their unwashed pits and other body parts. These guys were losers of the lowest order in my view, real human derelicts, human scavengers, or just plain refuse, but some might be of use to us, I realized. Peck recognized several of them and approached a small mixed-breed Indian - "breeds" they were called. This fellow looked to be about sixty years old and was known as "Broken-Nosed Joe", I suppose because his nose was bent way over to one side. Peck told the beed he needed some good workers for a couple of weeks - or longer if they were good workers. The pay was five dollars a day for regular hands, plus room and board, and ten bucks a day for experienced loose hay stackers.

Old Broken Nose Joe was just coming off a drinking binge, but he was pretty coherent. He was happy to see Peck and mentioned the good food and treatment he always got at Hound Creek. He said he was ready to go. Peck treated all his workers respectfully. He also tried to keep Boone Austin, the old fellow from the Elk Horn summer range from having too much contact with any of the Indians. Boone seemed to hate all "indins".

Peck told Joe to take the sprout (that was me) and drag out about four more men who looked like they could carry their own weight and bring them to the stock truck. "But don't pick any G.D. Ethiopians," he warned. Peck referred to black people as Ethiopians, which I thought was an intelligent way to get around the common epithet for negroes. I don't recall ever seeing any negroes during my time in Montana, but I heard Peck use the term "Ethiopians" often. He obviously had no use for them.

Peck remained in the shotgun seat of the truck as Joe and I entered the bar. Nobody made a fuss over me being in there as a minor. It took a little while, but Joe enlisted a very stout white man and two tough-looking, scarred-up Indians to help gather up two more unknown, but physically impressive men. Those big fellows were too drunk to protest much and we soon had Joe and the other five men loaded in the back of the truck. Peck told me to get us back home before any of the derelicts in the back tried to get away or woke up and caused us any other grief. I drove us off down the road toward Ulm, then to Cascade. We crossed the Missouri River and headed for Hound Creek with our shanghaied crewmen for the next day, or if they proved up, the coming month or more, of haying. We wound up with an extra hand or so, but Peck said maybe some of them might not work out and would have to be taken back to town - that usually was just to Cascade, if he fired them - besides, he could keep them all busy if they were worth keeping. Peck mentioned that it cost the ranch about a hundred dollars a day to operate during the haying season - three thousand a month! That seemed like an impossibly huge expense to me, but that was way back in 1958.

It had been a really interesting day for me!

## SHOWING PROMISE

I was hoping Broken Nosed Joe would be quartered with me, but reckoned it best to make no mention of it, as it wasn't my decision to make. Stan and Peck, like all my family, were unassuming people, and presumptuousness on the part of others was not appreciated or well tolerated. So, I said nothing about my preference for roommates, as it might lead to an uncomfortable reaction from either or both of them.

Stan and I serviced the big truck and did some work on other equipment preparing for the next day and I headed back to the cabin after dark. I was sure happy to see Joe snoring in what had been Eddie's bunk. Neither Stan nor Peck was obvious about it, but it seemed they were looking out for me, kind of. As time passed, Broken Nose Joe seemed to take a liking to me and told me a lot of interesting stories about how it was to be an Indian and how cute some of the little squaws in his tribe were. He offered to introduce me to some cuties. I was ready to go teepee creeping at the first opportunity, but no chance came my way. Anyway, I liked Joe and we got on very well together.

Well, one of the unknown drunks proved to be just no good at all, so Peck took him back to friend Bill's service station in Cascade. The guy could hitchhike from there. The rest of the men knew ranch work and were ready to dry out long enough to get more money for booze and smokes, so we were putting up hay about as fast as could be. One fellow got a little crude at dinner one night, Peck told him that crudeness and lack of civil manners would not be tolerated at Hound Creek and that was that. Everyone was on good behavior and avoided profanity, except for a "damn" or "hell" when outside and clearly out of hearing range of the women. It was a different story at the Whitmore place where the local manager was himself a loser and commonly used foul language wherever he happened to be.

Whitmore main house with bunkhouse in the back. It was a nice place, but the water always tasted foul.

The Whitmore barn was newer and bigger than the barn at Hound Creek

Whitmore Ranch had a great quonset and calving shed.

In the bunkhouse, especially at the Whitmore place, it was an entirely different situation. The Whitmore bunkhouse was occupied, at times, by up to a dozen or more men, none of whom were very admirable. Most of the "breeds" had bad facial scars and such, indicating they were probably barroom brawlers. I was happy to have my semi-private quarters while I was at Hound Creek. I did not enjoy the brief stints I did at the Whitmore place, but most of the horses and the one team of mules there were great to deal with.

With a full crew, most of whom knew and preferred gas-powered machines over horsepower, I got to work the dump rake teams most of the time, which was clearly my preferred job. I would drop the dump rake head with a foot release and drag the freshly cut hay along until time to deposit it in a wind row. After time for the cuttings to dry enough, I would run the team down the windrow with a rake wheel on each side of the row, dropping the rake periodically to gather up a "bunch", (which rolled and turned the cut hay to dry it even more) then hit the trip and so on, until the row had become a line of bunches, which would be left to dry a bit longer. Occasionally I would have to drive down and turn the damp bunches over an extra time or two.

A section of a gunny sack on the nose kept the flies and other pestiferous insects at bay.

A dump rake from behind and the view from the rake teamster's seat. Boots and Freddy were one of the two fastest light horse rake teams.

Driving down a windrow to "bunch" the freshly cut hay.

When I tripped the head to dump a load of hay, every now and then, a rattlesnake would come up impaled on one or more tines, buzzing worse than a hive full of hornets. The horses could hear it and were experienced enough to be spooked - especially Pete and Freddy, but each gelding was teamed with a more level-headed mare that would settle down right away, so I would get them stopped, unhook the tugs and use a pair of short willow sticks I carried on the rake to remove the serpent. I was glad that none of the serpents came up within striking distance of my butt as I sat in the metal seat. I killed every one of those vipers and took their rattles, but I got the idea one morning that it would be fun to put one in with the hay to be dropped on the stack. I sure didn't want to see anyone hurt or accidentally bitten, so I cut the head off of one big rattler which was over four feet long and threw it on top of a bunch of hay at the end of one line. Of course, I cut the rattles off and put them in my shirt pocket. I was to switch over to the bull rake for the afternoon, so when I went to pick up a load to take to the stacker, I paid special attention to the one with the beheaded and "detailed" snake in it.

After dropping that special load on the stacker's head, I got off to have a drink from the common water jug as the new hay went onto the

31

stack. I lingered to watch what happened with the snake. As the hay fell onto the stack, the men saw the viper and bailed off that loose stack like parachute soldiers, hollering "Snake, Snake!" I thought of the 101st Airborne bailing out over Bastogne, but the stack wasn't too high yet - it was only about ten or twelve feet above ground level.

Nobody noticed my concealed smirking, but soon one of the men was back up on the stack, casting around for the dreaded serpent. After a few minutes of gingerly sorting through the hay with his pitchfork, the fellow reached down and picked up the snake. Without saying a thing, he bailed off the stack and walked over to Stan. When they met, the older, irritated guy said, "This damned viper has its head and rattle cut off !"

Well, I might have been born yesterday, but I'd stayed up most of last night. I realized that my little trick and gone bad and my butt was apt to get pounded big time over this, so I put my brain into high gear.

Trying to act interested, but not guilty, I took another swig of water which went down the wrong tube and nearly choked me. As I coughed it out, Stan brought the snake to me with the stacker man glowering behind him and asked if I knew anything about the headless snake.

It's always best to stick with the truth, or as close to it as circumstances permit, so I told them, "Well, I speared two buzztails this morning and when I got them off the tines, I cut their heads off, stomped the heads into the ground and tossed their carcasses behind the rig so the horses wouldn't hear or smell them", I replied loud enough for everyone to hear. I showed Stan the two rattles I had in my shirt pocket.

The stacker asked how the devil that one got in the hay, then.

"Well?" asked Stan.

"Durned if I know, but maybe a magpie or a weasel tried to pick it up and dropped it," I offered.

"Well, next time you go to all that trouble, go ahead and cut the snake up into short pieces, so nobody gets the idea you set them up, or they might get sore about it, understand? A man could break a leg bailing off a stack like that!" Stan said after a short pause to think it over.

"And be blamed sure you don't get bit yourself, Jake," he added.

The stacker man continued to give me a dirty look, but he turned and went back to work as he muttered about how he might have broken his leg or neck getting away from the snake. (Yeah, a dead snake, too - I thought to myself.) I had never thought of that possible scenario. Unforeseen consequences can be really uncomfortable, and some practical jokes can go too far.

That incident led me to decide not to prank around like that by putting snakes in the hay ever again. It was a neat idea that nearly backfired with bad final results. Once again, I was feeling really lucky.

It pleased me to be put back to using the light horse teams to cut and rake hay most of the time. I preferred that over running the bull rake, a tractor, or any other haying chore. I kind of wanted to try stacking for double the pay, but I loved the horses way more than the money and figured I'd have a heck of a time keeping up with the experienced, grown men on the loose stack. Plus it was really hard on the legs, walking in the loose hay all day long. Also, the one old boy just might take delight in "accidentally" running a pitchfork through my belly, as I never did believe he bought my snake story. He was an unhappy, resentful sort and had no sense of humor, or so it seemed to me. He only stayed on the ranch for another week or so. He collected his pay in cash and walked to the road with his thumb in the air, looking for a ride, probably to someplace he could buy smokes and booze.

But boy, did I feel good driving those horses.

"Your folks sent me a boy and I'll send 'em back a man", Stan told me one evening in the shop as we were working on equipment needed for the next day.

"No, you won't, not until I'm ready to stop being a boy. I'm enjoying this time way too much to change," was my response. Besides, I thought his unoriginal comment had been a little overused in the movies and I was going to take credit for at least some of my own youthful thinking and actions.

Manhood, I figured, was not something that came with the passage of time... a birthday or such. I knew several adult males that I sure would hesitate to call men. Manhood and the respect it commanded, had to be earned. I aspired to it but knew I hadn't earned mine - not quite yet.

Stan stood only a little over five feet tall, but was as independent, feisty, and tough as anyone I had ever known - I so admired all the fight in that little dog uncle of mine - way more than I did the bigger combatants in some fights. I thought maybe I had some of the same genes. I loved my uncle as I did my Dad, but I would sure as heck never express that to him in words. Stan practiced tuff love and that always worked well with me, too. At his five feet four inches, Stan always stood real tall in my view.

After an especially productive day, Peck would sometimes meet with the crew outside the cookhouse and pull the cork on a bottle of hundred-proof Old Grand Dad bourbon, then he would pass the jug around for everyone to have a snort after supper, including me. Ready or not, I was beginning to feel like a man all right. I figured I would eventually merit that distinction - maybe sooner than most young fellows.

## FINALLY, ELKHORN AND REAL COWBOYING

Peck decided that it was time to check on the cattle and horses on the summer range. That was Elkhorn, and he told me to get ready to go up for a few days with Stan. I'd been hearing tales of Elkhorn from Stan since I was a baby and now I was finally going to get to see and experience it. I could hardly wait.

We left before daylight the next morning, with Stan driving the Jeep pickup, me riding shotgun, and Pooch, the border Collie, in the back. The cook had put together a food box with bacon, eggs, sausage, spuds, rice, beans, bread, flour, and other staples as well as some fresh cookies and a couple of pies. She even threw in some recent detective and Western magazines that she'd already read for old Boone to peruse. I don't recall any salad, but I didn't care about that. It was meat, potatoes, bread and butter for most working men and boys in those days.

The road was muddy, steeply side-hilled, and slick in places. We slipped and spun our muddy way into the mountains without serious mishap.

Grover Boone Austin was asleep in the musty, smelly old cabin when we arrived. Right away he got some coffee going and we had a second breakfast. Boone was eighty-eight years of age and soon after we met he told me that he had killed more than three dozen red-hide Indians in his earlier years. It was 1958 and I realized it could have actually been true. He often used the term "red-hide niggers", which was in common use in rural Montana back then.

Stan told me not to believe everything that old reprobate said, but Boone's monologue was nearly continuous and I was all ears. Stan maintained a demeanor of detached indifference to the old self-proclaimed Indian fighter.

Incidentally, Boone mentioned to Stan that he thought he had seen some pink eye in the herd, so we'd better keep a close watch out for that.

The Elkhorn cabin was said to have been built in the 1870s by a homesteader that most likely hunted elk to sell.

The barn at ElkHorn was newer and in far better shape than the cabin - which
is not unusual for buildings of conscientious, but low-budget stockmen.

Stan and I put our extra clothes and some personal stuff in the old
cabin, tying our sleeping bags and small personal kits, including tooth-
brushes, on behind our saddles for the next trip.

The cabin reeked of damp paper, mildew, dirty clothes, and whatever
else I couldn't even guess. It had been accumulating odors for over eighty
years and I figured most of the vapors had not improved with age. Its
smells were in noxious contrast to the green Montana grass. The old cabin
was clearly stale rather than fresh, but it wasn't as rank with human stench
as the Whitmore bunkhouse. Empty Bull Durham sacks and the remains
of other roll-your-own smokes were littered everywhere. There were plenty
of signs of rats and mice amidst the clutter of old magazines and pocket
novels. Rodent droppings were everywhere, including inside the bedding.
The mattresses had holes chewed in them, so their stuffing added to the
litter. Some areas showed bird droppings, too, so there must be some pretty
good-sized holes somewhere in the place. I dreaded our return when I
would no doubt the be one assigned to cleaning up that over-ripe pigsty.
I never liked doing housework but, I was resolved to do it if so ordered.

The place needed airing out, but Stan told me not to leave the door
or window open while we were gone as there were plenty of bears around
and we didn't want to share quarters with any bruins. That seemed like
a good idea to me.

We saw plenty of bear signs which included poop, clawed-up places in the ground, and scratches on corral posts and trees just about every day and everywhere we went. Peck's policy was to shoot every bear he could and Stan was of a similar mind on that and most issues. A good number of black bears met their end on that ranch. I hoped I could be the one to kill the next bear, but I expected one of the other more experienced, hands would get the job. But I still yearned for the chance.

The horses had already been corralled by Boone, so we were soon ready to head out to inspect the range cattle and scrutinize the stock for pinkeye. Stan and I each led a pack horse loaded with salt blocks and some medicines, along with our gear and some food. We could switch to riding either pack horse if necessary. Stan did all the horseshoeing for the ranch. He broke all the horses, too, and he had most of them trained to do multiple duties.

Boone rode his own horse, a tall black gelding named Mike. The name had great personal significance for Boone, which I came to understand later.

Now, finally, it looked like I was in for some of the real cowboy action that I had dreamed about for years.

Stan said I was to ride a big, tall, chestnut mare named Goldie. She was one of the smartest and best at roping and cutting of all the horses in the string. And she was the best broodmare, having fouled Babe, Ruben, and other fine horses, but she was as big as a barrel around the middle. After a day on her back, I felt like I'd been halfway drawn and quartered by professional torturers of the Spanish Inquisition. My butt felt like it was split an extra two inches up the natural crack, but Goldie was gentle and really knew her business, and she was fast and could turn sharp. I really loved her, even as I staggered around and had to duck-walk after being on her back for a few hours. Stan took a lanky black gelding named Silk which he told me was given to "salty" episodes at times, so I should avoid using him until I'd gained more experience in the saddle. Before we had gone a mile, Silk tried to unload Stan. Stan droped the lead rope for the pack horse and I retrieved it to hold while he sorted out Silk. Boone and I got a pretty good three or four-minute show as Stan spurred and bucked the ornery out of Silk. When he was done, Silk was lathered up and seemed to have aged considerably in the last few minutes. I thought I detected a submissive attitude in him, as well. It seems some horses, just like some people, never take to being good all the time and have to be chastised every now and then.

We rode down to what they called the Furrier Place, named for the original homesteader, I suppose. It was where most of the two and three-year-old steers were summering. We checked cattle for pinkeye and general appearance as we went along the way. Shortly after midday, Boone noticed a steer with a nasty-looking eye. Stan roped and threw that big three-year-old critter and I learned about "doctoring" for pink eye. It was pretty basic. A little tablet was placed in the affected, usually pus-rimmed, eye after any foxtail, burdock, or other irritants were removed. Then an antibiotic injection was given in the critter's rump. Stan gave the first shot, then he had me do the rest that day. This was the first of thousands of shots I would give, both as a wannabe cowboy and later as a dentist. I always tried to do them as painlessly as possible, even for the cattle. I would hit the target area a few times with my fist, then plunge in the needle. The innoculee never seemed to notice the stick. I developed a different, more gentle technique for dental patients, though. For people, I just wiggled their cheek, rather than hit them with my fist. The wiggling or pounding seemed to overload their sensory receptors, making the needle prick imperceptible or at least it was suitably masked.

We found and doctored eight steers with pinkeye that day. We washed our hands when we were close to a creek or seep, but we never had rubber gloves or disinfectant soap. Most of the time we did not wash at all unless we were at the headquarters and scrubbed up a little before supper. None of us developed pink eye, but we, like almost everybody I suppose, had all had the disease as children, so we were likely immune.

After roping the first animal, Stan had me ride Goldie on the right side of the target beast as he came along the left and tossed or dropped his loop over the head. It was a pretty efficient operation, primarily thanks to Goldie's cutting horse smarts and Stan making Silk behave himself.

I was feeling like I actually might make it as a cowboy! After a couple of catches, Stan told me to get my loop ready and drop it over the head of the next one. Stan pointed his finger at a small two-year-old steer and I spurred Goldie on toward it. When I was within arm's reach of the animal, I dropped my loop over the running beef's head. So it was a natural and easy thing to do. As soon as the loop was around the neck I would take a couple of wraps of the rope around the saddle horn. Goldie would plant all her feet and sometimes, if we were on a run, the steer would be jerked right off his feet.

We spent the night in an ancient line shack which was even a bit less attractive and no less stinky than the main cabin, but it was a shelter, of sorts. The old corrugated tin roof kept the rain out and the log walls would discourage a bear - at least long enough to alert the human occupants. I figured this old shack must be a hundred years old, like most of the other outlying shacks.

Morning coffee boiled in a can, then Boone poured in some cold water to settle the grains and served it up. "Cowboy coffee" tasted just fine, and I still make it that way when in the field, sometimes even at home. We ate fried potatoes, eggs, pork sausage, bacon, biscuits, and gravy. No bacon grease was ever thrown out. It got sopped up with a piece of biscuit and swallowed. We stuffed our bellies as usual and were ready for whatever the day might bring. Usually, a breakfast like this meant we would do without anything like a "proper" lunch. I often had a cookie or two in my pocket, but I never saw any candy bars on the ranch.

We found only a couple of animals with pinkeye that morning. One cow had a long deep gash that needed closing, so we got her roped and thrown and I got instruction in closing wounds with light copper wire, as that was what was available. We bobbed her tail by cutting off the hair at the end, to make her easy to pick out as Stan said she would be sold in the fall because her injury might lead to other problems.

Stan decided since we were close to a dandy stand of lodge pole pine, we ought to cut and peel some for later transport to Hound Creek for use as replacement bull rake and stacker head teeth. With Eddie's driving, an extra number of rake teeth had been broken. Stan was never one to waste time or opportunities - a practice that I was learning to appreciate and to follow whenever I could.

One horse harness and a single tree had been left in the line cabin for skidding poles and Goldie knew her job dragging poles out of the dense pine stands. As Stan and Boone used double-bit axes to cut and partially peel poles, I chained four to six poles together and then hooked to the single tree and either led or drove Goldie out of the woods into the open grassy park by the old cabin. I would unhook the dragline, stack the poles and return for more. Stan planned for us to have about sixty poles ready before we rode back up to the main cabin. At eighty-eight years of age, Boone could chop poles as well as a young man. He made no big deal of any job, he just did it. I was amazed. That old man had so much grit! I figured it must be due to the mountain water he was drinking …. or maybe his friend's home-brewed whiskey.

At lunchtime we were laying around, half dozing by a beautiful clear mountain stream when a steer came up behind one of the tethered pack horses and jumped right up on his back. I was amazed to see the steer begin humping the cayuse. I figured the poor horse must be near terminally mortified.

"Hey, what's going on ?", I yelled.

Stan lifted the brim of his hat and asked what was the matter.

"Well, Stan, that steer is trying to hump the gelding pack horse - and they're both males ?"

"Yep, they are. They're animals and don't know no better and neither one is gonna get any real love anyway, so why the fuss? They aren't gonna produce a 'cowrse or a how, on that, you can bet, for sure ", he explained. He yelled at the steer to get out of there, then rolled over in an attempt to get a short nap.

"I see ya got a lot of learning to do yet, sprout," Boone told me as he chuckled and studied my wide-eyed reaction.

I was wishing I had my Brownie Box camera, but it was back in the main cabin. In those days there had never been much surplus money in my family to be used on frivolous things and to my regret photographs were not as high on the list of worthy expenditures as they surely should have been. I intended to make that used camera that I'd purchased for two dollars last a lifetime, so I seldom carried it, for the risk of damage, as well as the cost of photo development. Even black and white photographs seemed expensive. I never had a camera capable of making color photographs until I was out of dental school nearly eight years later. Now, I sure wish I had splurged on that issue, more than any other, and carried a camera everywhere, especially on days like that with the steer humping the horse.

I never saw such an event of animal perversion or interspecies "husbandry" again. Maybe that's just as well, but pornographic aspects notwithstanding, I wish I had that picture to show. Oh well, there's sure more than enough sexual and gender confusion around in the two-legged animal population today, anyway.

We got sixty-seven poles stacked and mostly peeled - all were straight and ten to twelve feet long with little taper and about a six to eight-inch diameter. The poles were partially peeled and piled before we went back to checking over the cattle again. A draw knife could be used along with a couple of sawhorses to complete the pole peeling later. Stan figured we'd missed half a dozen or so steers, but considering all, we'd done okay. We had to go on to other areas, including the big pasture north of the main cabin that held most of the bulls and cows.

To everyone's surprise and relief, we found not a single animal showing signs of pinkeye in that huge pasture! It was far away from the areas that held the cattle that showed pinkeye, so maybe some sort of natural quarantine was working. But of course, we didn't see each and every one of the critters in that vast area. Nevertheless, Stan figured it was going to have to be good enough. His usual measure of "good enough" was "as good as can be". The salt blocks got set out and we repaired several patches of the barbed wire fence that had been torn down by elk during the previous winter. Repairing barbed wire fences was not my favorite job, but it did get me out on the range and in the wild, which I enjoyed.

Each day, as we rode through different pastures we paid attention to the fences. Rocky Mountain elk (*Cervus elaphus nelsoni*) broke down a lot of fencing. I wondered if they were spooked by a bear or cougar, or just didn't care about the minor discomfort and lacerations caused by the barbed wire. Naaw, surely they could feel their hides being cut and torn! The ranch had some partial rolls of wire and staples left in handy places here and there, and we all carried a pair of wire pliers in our saddle pocket, so repairing holes in the fences could be done easily. That was just another chore that was done when, as, and where needed.

I found several impressive shed antlers and one big winter-killed six-point bull skull. I was dreaming of someday hunting elk in those wild mountains. But that opportunity never came my way.

Two days later, Stan, Pooch, and I were ready to head back to the Hound Creek headquarters. Stan did tell Boone that we'd need to come back up in a couple of weeks to check on the pink eye situation. That news pleased me immensely, as I was hoping I might get to come along. Yeah, more real cowboy stuff and maybe a chance to shoot a bear!

Peck was just tickled by the way the whole operation, especially the haying, was going. We never got an official day off, but on rare occasions, and only on Sundays after breakfast, Peck would tell the hands to take the rest of the day off for themselves. Most of the men would just go to their bunkhouses, play cards, smoke, and nap. Peck wouldn't let crewmen have booze while on the ranch, but occasionally a man would have a small secret bottle stashed with his gear. Some men read whatever comic books or old magazines were available. But I always had several interesting things outdoors to engage in when time allowed.

## ONE OF THOSE RARE DAYS OFF

There was a huge population of groundhogs, whistle pigs, or Marmots, as some people called them, on Little Hound Creek. Those in this area were yellow-bellied marmots (*Marmota flaviventris*). In most cases, the rodents caused no harm, as they prefer rocky areas, but occasionally they would dig a hole that a stock animal could step into, potentially result-ing in damage to a leg or foot. Peck didn't like anything that threatened his stock.

Mormon crickets (*Anabrus simplex*) were thick that summer. They can grow up to nearly three inches in length and are considered to be a pest. They're actually a variety of katydids or locusts. Boone told me that some local Indians ate the disgusting-looking bugs. Peck explained how back in the century before - it was in the late spring of 1848, the crickets appeared in large numbers, and by summer the Mormons' second-season crops down in Utah were being devastated by a massive swarm of these insects until, according to a Mormon neighbor's story, large numbers of seagulls flew in on June 9 after fervent prayers for salvation by the Latter-Day Saints. The gulls ate a lot of the bugs, enough to save the Mormons' crops. The Mormons considered that insect disaster to be of Biblical proportions, referring to it as the eighth plague of locusts. The California gulls ate so many of the locusts, that the survival of four thou-sand Mormon pioneers was ensured. The miracle of the gulls is forever commemorated in a monument in Salt Lake City.

A Mormon Cricket

Sea Gull Monument in Salt Lake City, Utah.

Unfortunately, however, Mormon crickets do not make good trout bait.

One Sunday, Peck asked if I'd mind catching some grasshoppers - not Mormon Crickets, mind you, real grasshoppers - for his wife, Vera, to go fishing with, and then maybe I could try my hand at shooting and trapping some groundhogs. He said the ranch would provide traps, a .22 rifle, and ammunition, and pay me fifty cents apiece for dead groundhogs. I just needed to bring in the right front foot of any whistle pig I killed. I could easily fit a dozen or so marmot feet into my deep jacket pocket. And if I got the chance to shoot any magpies, he'd pay ten cents each for them. I just needed to keep a right foot off each one. Magpies (*Pica pica*) get to pecking at wounds on a stock animal's back - so Peck didn't like them either. I thought I couldn't dream of a nicer way to spend a day off!

I gathered up a couple of dozen of the finest, liveliest grasshoppers you ever saw - or even imagined - and presented them to Vera, who invited me to join her for some native Rainbow Trout fishing. She loaned me her spare pole and some hooks. She showed me how to use a fly, but the live grasshoppers worked best by far. We fished for about an hour just in front of the cookhouse and caught ten fish that measured from twelve to sixteen inches in length and would make a nice special meal for Peck, Vera, Stan, and, by special, and rare, invitation ... me!

After carefully cleaning the fish I set off for real fun with the traps and rifle. I set the leg hold traps by entrances to marmot holes. No bait was necessary. These pests had been neglected too long and were pretty uneducated in the ways of people.

The first big boar groundhog I shot square in the chest, with a .22 long rifle bullet, but the hardy rodent made it into his hole. I was ashamed of myself for wounding an animal, then seeing it crawl off into a damp, dark hole to eventually die alone, and not be put to a useful purpose - which, in this case, was the fifty-cent bounty for me. Clearly, only head shots would drop the pigs and allow me to recover the carcass and remove a foot. After my first bungle, I made only head shots and never lost another whistle pig - but I did sometimes make a clean miss, which irritated me some.

Considering all, this seemed like appropriate stewardship to me.

Some of my first day's groundhog kills.

By evening I had trapped three and shot - and recovered - eight more groundhogs in about three hours of entertaining and stimulating activity. That was an extra five and a half dollars on top of the daily five bucks. I was being paid for doing what I loved best. And I knew it just doesn't get any better than that! I slept especially well that night.

Seventy cents worth of bonus varmints taken one evening after supper and chores.

Talk about hog, or groundhog heaven, I was living in it!

Vera's pan-fried trout dinner and the fresh pie were wonderful, along with the realization that I had made better than double wages that day ... for doing good and having fun! Yes, I was doing well by doing good. Gosh, I even felt like part of this family. Stan always referred to Peck as "Dad" Wareheim, but I didn't feel like I had the liberty to do that, plus I thought it might be somehow unfair or disrespectful to my own real Dad who was as good as they come.

## DREADING MY RETURN TO SCHOOL

We were into August already and I was trying to avoid thinking that soon I would have to honor my promise to Mom and return to high school. I would never have gone back on my word and Stan wouldn't have let me do it, even if I'd tried, but I tried to bury the thoughts of leaving the ranch. I was afraid that somehow I might never get to come back to that magical place. I had to concentrate on enjoying things as they came along and not dread the future, no matter how dismal it might look. I reminded myself that it's no good to make monsters in one's mind, as the world has enough real monsters already.

When I was just a little kid I learned to stop scaring myself by thinking about Lon Chaney morphing into a werewolf when I was outdoors alone at night. My self-advice was to "not make any monsters by fearing the unknown." I had learned to practice that successfully - most of the time. Nevertheless, I was sad about the prospect of going back to jail (high school), and even sadder about leaving the ranch. In truth, I felt that I would never leave the place, nor would it leave me. And more than sixty-five years later, I guess I never did leave, as it's still in my heart and mind.

Most of the hay was put up in loose stacks, but some of the scattered, smaller patches were more practical to bail. I liked handling bales as it was great exercise and baled hay sure was easier to transport than having to tear apart a loose stack with a pitchfork, throw it onto a wagon and pitch it off as the wagon rolled through the feeding ground. With bales, we just unloaded them off their stack, cut the wires or strings, and threw or pitch-forked the sections of hay where we wanted it to go. Sometimes Stan used the Farmhand to take bales off a stack and dump them on a wagon - that was a huge time and muscle-saving procedure.

But the loose stacks of hay did keep a lot better. It was greener, smelled better, and seemed noticeably fresher.

On each trip to the hayfields, or anywhere else, I was "all eyes" for whatever might present itself. Rattlesnakes were frequently seen and I killed all those that could be handily dispatched - which was most of the ones I came across. Sage grouse or Prairie Chickens were a delight to encounter, except for those times that they flushed right in front of the horses and spooked the team or the saddle horse I was on - which spooked me, too.

Some of the most intriguing critters for me were the Pronghorns (*Antilocapra americana*). Most days we would see a closely bunched herd of about ninety of them running through the hay field - they were gliding it seemed. It looked as if they were flying close to the ground.

Those animals seemed to move both legs on the same side at the same time, making their fast travel the smoothest I had ever witnessed in any animal. I never saw an antelope jump or bound like deer. Peck did not care for those "lopes" and referred to them as "plague-gone goats". He told me that they tasted like spoiled mutton and were worse than worthless, but we couldn't shoot them as pests, due to the fact that they were protected and the game warden would levy heavy fines on anyone who was caught taking Pronghorns illegally.

Antilocapra are swift.

I was highly motivated to shoot one someday, legally, to check out the meat and really give the carcass a thorough going over. I knew that they were unique to the "deer-like" family. Their Latin name is *Antilocapra* - the antelope goat. I found some horn sheaths in the fields that had been slipped off due, I supposed, to new horn growth. This is similar to the shedding of deer antlers. No other horned animals exhibit this natural process These critters fascinated me way beyond my usual state of sustained amazement. As for eating, lots of people in Arizona said Javelina was not fit for human consumption, but Mom could use spices to make it taste good. I was sure pronghorn meat would be just fine on the table if it was spiced up and prepared properly.

Finally, in 1987 I made an opportunity to hunt Pronghorns. I stopped off in Missoula on my drive from Alaska to Arizona and drove to Malta, Montana with a friend. After seeing about two hundred Pronghorns in three days and soaking up as much of their habits and the beautiful country as I could, I shot a decent buck and spent about two hours admiring, inspecting, and butchering the animal. The following day I simply prepared some of the meat. I just fried it and added some pepper and I found it to be good tasting.

A decent Pronghorn I shot near Malta, Montana in 1987.

Stan at the common water jug. The "Farm Hand" is in the background.

As for Peck's comments about the spoiled mutton flavor, I just wrote them off as cattlemen being cattlemen. Other people's opinions are sometimes best just left alone as they seem inscrutable to the rest of us and there's nothing to be gained by argument or debate. This is especially true with politics.

Along with the bales of hay came my introduction to the "farm hand". It was larger, but similar to the motorized bull rake in that it was built on a big truck chassis with dual power wheels in front and steering wheels behind. This gave the machine much greater maneuverability with quick turning and allowed the weighty load to be in front of the driver, and directly in front of the power wheels. While the bull rake only had a hand winch to raise and lower the teeth for picking up a load, the farm hand had a hydraulic system to raise, lower, and dump its loads. Talk about a labor-saving device!

The tines of the head of the Farmhand were lodge pole pine,
the same as those on the Bullrake and the stacker head.

A well-made stack of bales is impressive to most folks. Some of the bale stacks seemed to be as precisely built as the great pyramids.

A 118 bale load on the big Chevy

But my preference remained with driving or using horses in any manner, still, it is undeniable that this wonderful labor-saving machine, the Farmhand, was a lot of fun to operate, as well.

Stacking bales took no special skill, but they must be overlapped, or "tied in". I liked stacking bales because the seventy-pound bundles were great for building upper body strength, and after spending so much time in the seat of a dump rake, I felt like I needed that exercise.

## Bring 'em Back Alive

One afternoon as we were piling bales, I stopped for a pull on the common water jug and noticed a weasel nearby, I dropped the jug and ran after it. The little beast turned away from the cover as it humped and loped along in the stubble with me close behind. I took off my hat, made a dive, and had the critter pinned under my hat. I was wearing a pair of "railroader" gloves with cuffs to protect my forearms from being chaffed by the abrasive hay bales. That fierce little predator came up right through the top of my hat, scratched its way up my glove, and got inside the right cuff. It made a couple of quick rounds, practically girdling my forearm as one would a tree, then the little beast was out and ran into the bale stack and safety. Everyone saw my foolish escapade and when I pulled off the glove to inspect the remains of my bleeding arm, the men broke into a hearty guffaw.

My arm was leaking my vital life juices from a multitude of little claw scratches.

"Well, Bring 'Em Back Alive, what are you going to try next ", asked Stan?

Ignoring the question and laughter, I put my now much holier hat back on, took another swig of water, tried to act nonchalant, and went back to stacking bales without comment. If that ten-ounce bundle of furry dynamite had been a little bigger, maybe I wouldn't still even have an arm or remained alive. Truly, weasels are ferocious, but so very admirable!

## END OF SUMMER IN SIGHT

The end of August was rushing toward us and I kept dreading my departure when Stan and I made the second trip to Elkhorn. The plan was to check again for pink eye and bring back a bunch of cull cows that Boone had cut out of the pastured herd. The Staunton Ranch Company had registered Herefords so Peck and Stan were very selective on which got culled. Linebackers and rednecks, simply due to their unapproved hide markings were not used for breeding. Their sole function in life was to eat, stay healthy and make beef.

So why would the markings have any effect on the quality of the beef? I wondered about that, however, my lot was not to wonder why, but just do and try not to die. In 2009 when I took Stan's ashes back to Hound Creek, I saw only black Angus cattle, which reportedly produced better-tasting beef. That's a good reason, but the color marking is not!

When we reached the summer place, Boone said he had seen a big black bear boar close by the house, but he had not been able to get a shot at it. I dreamed of such an opportunity and Stan had let me carry his 30-40 Craig, just in case. It sure looked nice in the saddle scabbard, but that's where it stayed. Maybe someday, I'd bust a bear, I reckoned.

We spent six wonderful days at Elkhorn and departed one fine morning down the forty or so miles to Little Hound Creek with a little more than forty culls. We moved the cattle as slowly as possible to minimize stress and "shrink". We would stop at the creeks for them to fill up, wanting to keep their weight up and stress down. Now and then one of the jugheads in the herd would try to take off, so Stan would sic Pooch on the errant bovine. On rare occasions, either Stan or I would have to ride after an escaping beef. On a few occasions we would lose a half hour or more getting the mob back together and moving, but most of the time it was leisurely cowboying. How I loved that kind of trip!

Once we got the cattle out of the open, mostly unfenced country in the summer range, trailing down the roads was easy. Moving cattle along a road with fences along both sides kept the wannabe runaways in line with the rest.

Out of the mountains and trailing down the county road.

This trip took two days and it was easy herding, with the border collie, Pooch, doing his job so well. I wished it would never end. We slept on our saddle blankets with our "sleeping roll" (a wool blanket) thrown over our clothes. That was plenty good enough in the late summer and early fall weather.

We put the culls in the pasture called the "Dipping Vat" section and went to supper.

The haying had gone as good as could be, but it subtracted time from riding fences and other more entertaining "cowboy" things. And time was approaching for me to head back to high school. Ratz! I deaded the thoughts of school!

## LEAVING THE LITTLE BELT MOUNTAINS FOR THE ARIZONA DESERT

The much-dreaded day came and I packed a box to leave with Stan for my hoped-for use next season. In addition to some clothes, it included my chaps, those pointy-toed cowboy boots, spurs, a one-ear hackamore bridle, leather jacket, redwing knock-off lace boots, some pairs of half-used-up gloves, and a few other small items. I hadn't accumulated many material things, but with my five dollars a day and the bounty from groundhogs and magpies, I'd saved up close to five hundred dollars, I'd learned a lot, and I had stored some unique memories that would last a lifetime - because I figured they had to last forever. I planned to be a better all-around hand next summer.

Vera had to see a doctor in Great Falls, so Peck, Vera, and Stan saw me off at the airport after a big steak dinner at midday. I don't remember a thing about the airplane flight to Tucson. I was feeling really low and I think I must have dozed most of the way.

## MY JUNIOR YEAR IN HIGH SCHOOL

But school looked and seemed different. I never needed to do much, if any, homework, but I did pay attention to the teachers that I respected and those that seemed to enjoy teaching - and we had a few exceptional dandy instructors. I learned that by staying alert enough in class, there was no need to do any homework. My grades had always been nearly straight A's, in spite of myself.

And I continued to run to and from school almost every day. When I heard of a cement pour I would ask for the leftovers and make heavier barbells and other exercise gear.

And nobody said anything to me about my "weak" heart very often anymore.

I kept getting the double Bicillin shots, one in each cheek, every month. But they didn't hurt at all. I had become nearly immune to pain, or so I told myself. That helped a lot on those infrequent occasions when I got smacked hard in a fistfight.

Frequently I would get sharp pains in my left upper chest area, but I never told anyone about that. They most often occurred when I was not actively engaged in strenuous physical activity. In retrospect, I believe the chest pains were psychosomatic. I figured they were just in my head and I stuffed them into that "back room" of my mind where I put things I couldn't or didn't want to deal with at the time. That back room has saved me from a lot of unwarranted worries over the years, and it still does.

The physical demands of the ranch work had bulked me up some and the school's super athletes just didn't mess with me much at all that year. More than that, I think they knew if they did antagonize me, they'd have a fight on their hands. My last two years in high school were punctuated with only a few pugilistic bouts - and those, of course, only with opponents who really deserved it. However, I was never one to put up with being bullied or seeing anyone else abused in my presence. I just wouldn't tolerate it. I interceded on behalf of other victims on several occasions, and I do so to this day. One kid in my class, I'll call him Eric, looked like he might be in sixth grade. He was small in size, had a baby face, and was always nice to everyone. A couple of habitual bullies in our class liked to bump into Eric as they walked by him. Sometimes they would knuckle-thump him on his head, just for fun. When I noticed that, I told the bigger of the two that if either of them bumped or thumped Eric again, I was going to tear into them - both of them. I've always been blunt. If I were smarter, I maybe could have phrased it in a less provocative way, but I spoke from the heart and when the bigger of the two guys took a swing at me, I dodged his punch and caught him squarely in mid-gut. He staggered back and I gave him another swift punch to the belly.

He just doubled over and again I told him to lay off Eric. My face was lobster red and I was angry.

As bad luck would have it, a real sissified male teacher (he was wearing sandals which were thought to be extremely sissified in 1958 !) saw the end of our exchange and we both had to report to the office. Eric followed along behind and when we got interrogated over why we were fighting, Eric told his side of the story. We were warned, but not kicked out of school.

In 2007 at our forty-seven-year school reunion, I had a chance to have a drink with Eric. He looked like he might be in his early to mid-forties and commented, "Jake, my youthful looks plagued me before, but they're sure paying off now".

"Let's drink to that,", I said.

It was enjoyable to engage with schoolmates at "kid dances" and other social events, most of which were sponsored by one church or the other. I did not join a church, as I figured I was too young and inexperienced to make such a big decision, so I attended every church in town at one time or another. The activities and especially the pretty girls were what drew me to the services, but I had no doubts whatsoever about God and the blessings He continued to bestow upon me, for which I thanked Him every day.

There were square dances which I liked the best of all the kid activities.

The Mormon Church had good dances and I never saw any drinking or ornery behavior at any of their shindigs. I was a frequent guest at Latter Day Saints doings and a member of their Boy Scout troop. The scoutmaster, Mister Eldon Porter, was a Bishop in the church, as well. He was a fine man and leader.

But my main interest, aside from ranching in Montana, was always hunting.

Once in a rare while, I would find an interesting girl that would go hunting with me, but only for birds or rabbits. I was disappointed with the girls who would lament the killing of a wild animal but then went to the store to buy domestic meat without a qualm. I told them that I would far rather be a wild critter with a chance of eluding a hunter than a domestic animal, raised purely for meat and headed for the slaughter-house after a short period of eating, making meat, and getting hormone shots, with no real chance of any other destiny.

My Dad and I enjoyed some really good deer hunts. We didn't get any big trophy bucks that year, but we put meat on the table and enjoyed each other's company, as always. I missed a huge Mulie buck that erupted from a patch of bear grass between me and Pop, and I sure was deflated over that. The buck broke cover only a few yards from us and I shot over the top of him.

Early one morning we were positioned in a spot to look over the scrub oak, mixed woodland habitat below us when my Dad spotted a mountain lion. The big cat was traveling up country, toward us, but its path would keep it well out of range of our rifles. We were impressed by how the animal would speed up as it crossed open areas, then slow to creep along in the brush. Seeing a wild mountain lion in Arizona in 1958 was a pretty rare event. We found a nice buck Coe's deer skull with part of the hide still on and the nasal bones chewed up, which is typical for lion-killed deer. Of course, I packed the skull and antlers home. The local game warden told me that a mature lion has to eat a deer every week or so to survive. With fewer lions, there would be more deer to hunt and eat. I resolved to hunt lions in the future. The following week a fellow down the street from us got a cougar, so I took Gram over to see the big cat.

We each got a wild turkey that autumn my sister got one too, along with dozens of Gambel Quail, Mourning Doves, and a few puddle ducks, most of which we jump shot at cattle tanks (watering ponds for range cattle) and I kept Mom supplied with as many cottontails as we and the neighbors cared to eat. I preferred wild rabbits to domestic chickens, as many of our neighbors did after being exposed to wild rabbit flesh.

Gram admires the neighbor's freshly killed Tom Cougar.

In spite of the activities, the year seemed to go along slowly. My heart was at the ranch, wondering what was going on, how my favorite horses and Pooch dog and old Boone were doing, and most of all wondering if and when I would ever get back.

But I studied dutifully during my junior year in high school, completing all my course requirements early, including my term paper on the Abominable Snowman, which in some parts was known as the Yeti or Sasquatch. It seemed odd to me that so little physical evidence of these wild men had been collected and I was resolved to shoot one if ever a chance came my way. I kept my grades up, motivated primarily by my hope and expectation of departing early from the cactus-ridden desiccated desert of southern Arizona for the so much more interesting and fertile country in the great northwest. My sacrifices and diligence did pay off and I was allowed to skip out of school a couple of weeks before the last class roll call had been taken. However, my departure was done with the somewhat begrudging approval of the school authorities. And I really didn't give a hoot about what they thought about that. It was up to me to make it in life or not and I never doubted that I would make it.

Montana was calling and I was eager to get back to her. I wanted to get to take part in opening up the mountain pastures and cabin, riding the fences to repair elk damage to the barbed wire, branding the last of the new crop of calves, and so many other things I would miss if I didn't get there before June rolled up on the calendar.

Finally, the month of May 1959 arrived. My grades were excellent, thanks mostly to my motivation to return to Montana and my good teachers. My compulsive nature has always led me to get the job done now - or as soon as possible - to avoid having to do it later.

## BACK TO THE LITTLE BELTS

On my departure day, I ran home at three o'clock in the afternoon, grabbed my bag, and told Gyp, our devoted little dog since he wandered into our yard and lives back at the Trench Mine, I would miss him. Pop drove me to Tucson, where I boarded the DC3 at seven o'clock that evening, bound for the Little Belt Mountains and Little Hound Creek via Denver, Casper, Billings, and Great Falls. I really enjoyed what little flying I had done. And all the stewardesses I encountered were young, pretty, and seemed to me to be flirtatious in those days. Of course, maybe I was just engaging in the daydreaming of an average teenage boy regarding the flirting part.

The milk run plane departed Billings just as the sun was coming up. I saw the Yellowstone River shining in the early morning light and daydreamed of what it would have been like to have seen it with Lewis and Clark in 1805. That was only a hundred and fifty-four years earlier. I knew their story almost as well as if I had been with them and I wished I had been along on that extended trip. That was clearly the absolutely greatest adventure of all time, in my view.

One of my most common boyish daydream wishes was to have been born a hundred or two hundred years earlier. Maybe I would have been with George Washington at Trenton, Andy Jackson at New Orleans, or General Lee in the Wilderness battle. Better still, I might have been one of the old mountain men, attending the annual Big Hole rendezvous and living off the land. I figured I might have been exploring Kentucky and skirmishing with Cherokee Indians. I could have been helping settlers cross the great plains en route to the Oregon Territory, as my great grand uncle, Ben Michael, had done. I might have been fighting Blackfeet, as Boone Austin told me that he and his brothers had done for many years. Or I could have dealt with Apaches in southern Arizona and New Mexico, where my Dad and I had found arrowheads, broken pottery, and other artifacts as we hunted deer, javelina, and other animals.

I had often daydreamed of being a Professional Hunter in East Africa like the guy I saw in the movie <u>King Solomon's Mines</u>, which is still one of my favorite movies.

It would have been a great, adventurous life. Yeah, I dreamed of grand adventures - not so much as a leader, but just as a participant. But, as I consoled myself, so far my life was turning out pretty darned good, anyway.

## A DIFFERENT WELCOME, 1959

Stan was there to meet me at the Great Falls airport, with the usual cigarette hanging out of the corner of his mouth. He had been a two-pack-a-day man since he was sixteen years old. Uncle Stan passed away in 2007 at age eighty-two, still smoking and cancer-free as far as we knew. In spite of his smoking, he still had plenty of power and stamina in both body and spirit.

This time he greeted me with a hearty handshake, instead of a punch in the chest, and said we were going to go get some breakfast at Black Eagle. Wow, I had already eaten what the pretty young airline stewardess gave me and I wondered why Stan would waste his money on a restaurant? Oh well, if he wanted to do it, I was going to join him with no argument or comment, other than a hearty thanks.

And what a breakfast it was! We had steak and eggs, hash browns, sausage, coffee, and orange juice with a double order of whole wheat toast on the side. My stomach felt overstretched, but I knew it would accommodate the load, and my gut needed to get back into stretched, working condition. This little cafe had a selection of really good jams like blueberry, strawberry, and blackberry, not just the darned grape jelly. It's always seemed to me that everybody leaves the grape spread sitting for whoever comes along next, but most select the better stuff.

Stan asked if I'd had enough. I told him I was stuffed like a turkey and I'd get the tip. I'd been making more money mowing lawns in

Arizona than I did at five dollars a day on the ranch, but I'd take the ranch life every chance I got.

"No, you won't. It was my idea, it's on me and that's that," Stan said. Most everything was final with Stan. He wasted little time on unnecessary debates or palavering.

We drove back to "the Falls" and stopped off at the cowboy general store to pick up some supplies for the ranch. Stan asked me how much my feet had grown. Well, I wasn't about to get pushed into buying another overpriced pair of pointy-toed cowboy boots like the year before, so I told him they hadn't grown at all, seemed like they were done growing - might have shrunk, even.

"You right sure about that ?" Stan asked with eyebrows raised, indicating he wasn't convinced.

"Right sure," I replied, wanting to save that twenty-two dollar expense, and hoping the year-old cowboy boots would still fit. And if they didn't fit, I could suggest that the boots had shrunk in the cold Montana winter. It would be worth a try, anyway.

I did get a couple of pairs of leather work gloves and, for a dollar, three big colorful handkerchiefs to use as bandanas.

By then, it was noon, so Stan and I ordered cheeseburgers at a downtown hotel, even though I wasn't at all hungry. It was the place where all the ranch people came when in the big town. It was the place to be if one was in the local ranching business. Several men came over to talk with Stan. He introduced me as his nephew, which got me a series of firm handshakes and approving smiles. It was obvious that everyone who knew Stan held him in high regard.

As we left the hotel, Stan said a new John Wayne movie was playing, so maybe we ought to go see it. A movie? I was flabbergasted !

"What about all the work we have to do ?", I asked.

"We'll get caught up in the next couple of days or so," he replied.

The Horse Soldiers with John Wayne was the most enjoyable movie I had seen in a long time.

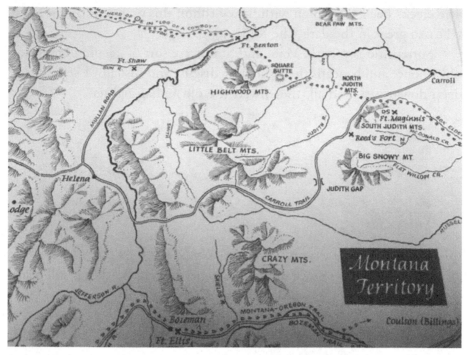

I copied this map showing our area from a book that Peck had called "Before Barbed Wire". It shows the country accurately.

On the way back to Hound Creek, Stan filled me in on how the winter had been, and how the calving went, including a story about a two-headed calf that had been born alive and died in a few minutes, short stories about some of the horses I had used - all of which had wintered well. He mentioned folks I had met who died that winter and other information on people and critters I knew.

I asked about Boone.

"Aw, that ole reprobate is healthier than his horse, besides, eighty-nine years old or not, he's way too ornery to die. Oh, yeah, he asked about you a few times. He'll probably come down from his squatter's cabin in Squaw Hollow where he always holes up for the winter to have supper with us tonight, so you can talk to him yourself, You might have to put up with him in your cabin if it gets too late for him to ride home.

The creek's been awful high with heavy runoff this year, and Boone's eyes aren't so great in the dark," he told me.

Surreptitiously, Peck, Vera, and Stan were sort of keeping an eye on old Boone, and beneath their show of disgust and disdain, I sensed that deep down, each and all, they loved the old Indian fighter.

The winter had been a tough one and some of the range stock was still being fed at Hound Creek

Using the farm hand to load a horse-drawn feed wagon with hay from a stack saved a lot of time and muscle work.

The winter of 1958-59 had been a long, cold one with especially heavy snowfall in the Little Belt Mountains. Then spring came a little late, for which I was thankful. I wondered what Elkhorn would be like.

The county road to the ranch was normally well maintained, but the spring thaw had been late. The county road crew was late with their maintenance and the road was deeply rutted. The ruts and the gumbo mud made for a slow trip. The steel bridge about a mile upstream from the ranch headquarters had some logs and brush stuck in the lower girders indicating very high water had recently flooded the creek bottom. But it all looked absolutely beautiful to my desert-accustomed eyes.

And there were those wonderful smells! No place I've ever been smells as good as Montana in the springtime. I felt like I was coming home. And I was back!

Peck and Vera came out of the main house to greet me and Vera fussing that old Boone would probably be late and likely drunk, as she went back in to finish up supper. It was her style to be fussy. The haying crew and summer cook hadn't come to work yet, so Vera did the vittles, as she referred to meals. It looked like it was going to be just Peck, Stan, Boone, and me at Hound Creek for a while. I wondered what new jobs they would be breaking me in on. I figured the time would be full of wonder for me.

Stan told me to stow my stuff in my cabin and change into working clothes as the cow needed milking before we ate.

"Reckon you can remember how to milk?", Stan asked.

Milking a cow was one of the few ranch or farm things that I hadn't learned here, as I had been milking since I was about five years old back in Iowa - and I always enjoyed it.

"Well, I sure will try to remember," I assured him. I'd learned to appreciate the importance of being humble and unassuming - even if it was affected.

So, I dropped my stuff off at the little log cabin. Right off, I noticed it smelled nice inside. Somebody had even put a scented candle in there. That must have been Vera, though she never would admit to it. The cabin was clean and my box of stuff was already there, with my chaps and spurs thrown over the end of my bed. I nearly had a tear form in both eyes! I bit my lower lip to keep it from showing. I was overjoyed!

This was sure different from my first day at Hound Creek the year before! This year I didn't wind up on the ground at the Great Falls airport, after a hard thump, for starters!

As I stripped the cow's tits to finish off the milking, I heard a raspy cough. Boone was there, standing with one arm on the stanchion. His horse, Mike, was standing by the door.

"Howdy Boone blamed good to see you," I said, trying to talk the local lingo.

He spit out a nasty, slimy wad of tobacco and said, "Well I heard that you wuz gonna be driving teams again this summer and might even have some interest in real cowboy activities up at the Elkhorn, so I figured I oughta come to see if it was the truth or not".

"It's true, and you can bank on it," I assured him.

When I took a few steps to shake his tobacco-stained hand, he said: "Well, Sprout, it looks like you growed some, too."

"Naw, not too much, Boone," I replied.

"Well, you better be sure to clean up good for supper. That Vera, she don't like dirty hands or faces at her table and I heared she made sumthin' special for tonight. Even sent Stan up the creek to give me an invite, which ain't common, so I rode old Mike down from Squaw Holler. Mike don't like extry fuss no more. Took an extry hour or so to make the ride, what with dodging downed trees and log jams in the crossings. Why, last week I even come close to running out of snoose, so I went to Red Man chew. The durned creek was so high last week it would have been a swim instead of a ride. Today I had to buck some logs off'n the trail and this week I'm gonna be busy with a saw and ole Mike dragging limbs and clearing the way. If'n a feller was a wee bit tipsy negotiating that route, he jest might find hisself in a wreck, " he offered as he took another big pinch of his loose-leaf chewing tobacco.

Boy, it was good to see old Boone. His real name was Grover Boone Austin. His brother whom he said was killed by Blackfeet Indians was named Mike. Just about every important thing that Boone owned, namely his rifle, his horse, his dog, his cat, and even his dilapidated old truck was named Mike. I never heard that he ever had a wife or a woman companion.

I told Boone that there was plenty of room in my cabin for him to stay as long as he wanted and he was welcome, anytime.

"Well, we'll scrutinize the necessary for that later, Sprout, but you hustle that milk along, cuz it's nearly supper time, and ya know ya better not keep that Vera waiting," he said.

A lot of the old boys like to use impressive words like scrutinize, libations, and such. I guess it was entertaining for them. Maybe they thought it was showing off their smarts or something like that.

As we visited I would frequently squirt one of the several barn cats that were hanging close with a shot of fresh milk, right out of the cow's tit. The cats shuffled around to get in position for their dose. After a shot of milk they fastidiously wiped off their faces with their tongue, then their paws. I supposed that even as fussy as Vera was, she would approve of that clean-up.

The three-gallon milk pail was filled close to the brim, so I carried it slowly, ever so carefully, followed by several of the younger barn cats, some still licking their faces, to the spring house which sat at the base of the hill next to the main log house where Peck and Vera lived. The natural flow of spring water kept everything nice and cool in there - even on hot summer days. What milk wasn't used by the cooks got slopped to the pigs after the next pail or two was squeezed out of the cow. Nothing got wasted. Sometimes neighbors would come over and take a pail or two of milk for their table needs.

Stan carries a pair of milk pails as he heads for the spring house and Pooch comes to check me out.

I heard Vera banging on the dinner bell and started at a trot, then I remembered that I ought to wash up. There was water already in the pitcher in my cabin, so washing up took only about two minutes.

My dash to the cook house put me right on the heels of Stan, so I knew I wasn't going to be too late!

Peck and Boone were already seated as Vera brought in a platter of big, thick, homegrown, Porterhouse steaks. There were two steaks for each of us. She had mashed potatoes - as always with plenty of gravy, a big fresh salad with lots of tomatoes, baked beans, and corn on the cob - where she got that corn so early in the summer, I couldn't guess. And I could smell her hot, deliciously spiced apple pie somewhere nearby.

I noticed that cramming extra high-calorie food down one's throat when a person is working hard doesn't seem to make them uncomfortable. It's just extra fuel going into the tank, and it will get used up soon enough.

Vera got herself seated and told Peck to offer the blessing. Peck suggested with a little cough and snicker, that Boone might want to do that.

Stan gave Boone a kind of odd look as Boone shifted in his chair.

"Well, Lordy, all a' us here sure do thank you for this here fine eatin' and all. Oh, thanks for the Sprout here, too. Good to have him back. I guess that's about it. Thanks again" was his prayer, which he followed up with wiping his whiskers, then wiping his hand on his pant leg.

We all said "Amen."

Vera glared her most poisonous, ornery look at Boone but said nothing.

Boone just stared at the pile of big, juicy steaks. A trace of brown snoose drool crept out of the left corner of his mouth.

That dinner went down wonderfully amidst talk of how the winter had been and plans to get up to Elkhorn with the first batch of cows and calves. Peck figured that the four of us, along with two dogs could do the first trip just fine. What a way to start the season. I was looking forward to that!

That special apple pie got served up with a big scoop of vanilla ice cream. Ice cream was something I had not seen or heard about at Hound Creek before that occasion.

I asked Vera if she could use some help with the dishes and she let me do them, as the men smoked and visited over the dinner table.

When I had the dishes all done and wiped down the table, Peck suggested we all might pour a little John Barleycorn down our necks before going off to bed.

Peck reached under his chair and brought up an unopened fifth of hundred-proof Old Grand Dad. He handed it to me first!

No way was I going to start it, as I figured I wasn't qualified.

"Sir, I would feel bad about being the first to pull on the brand new jug, would you please start it for us, Sir ?", I asked Peck.

"Heh, heh, Jake, you're reminding me of your uncle." He took a hearty swig and passed it back to me. I handed it to Boone, who without hesitation, poured enough down his pie hole to make the jug gurgle a few times before he handed it to Stan, who never was a heavy drinker. He took a respectful shot, then set it on the table next to me. I looked at Peck.

"Now it's your turn for sure, Jake."

"Yeah, Sprout, give 'er a good pull" was Boone's comment, which drew dirty snake-eye looks from both Stan and Vera.

So I stuck the bottleneck between my lips and turned the bottom up, but only took a little. Old Grand Dad was a good Kentucky bourbon and the only brand I ever knew Peck or Stan to drink. But it's a hundred proof - noticeably more powerful than the common eighty-proof stuff and I was a pretty inexperienced drinker.

I put the bottle back in front of Peck and thanked him as I wiped my lips off on my sleeve, as I had seen all the others do. Peck stuck the cork back in the bottle, signaling to all, especially Boone, that the drinking was over.

Stan said we had a full day coming, so he was going to turn in for the night. Boone glared longingly at the bottle but drew himself up out of the chair and headed for the door. Outside, Boone asked if the offer of him to overnight with me was still good.

"If I offer something, Boone, you can count on it. Besides, I've stayed at your place how many times? I'd welcome you anytime in my cabin, my friend," I happily assured him as I laid my hand on his shoulder.

In the cabin Boone told me that he figured once the seal was broke, a bottle should be finished, to make sure it didn't go bad on you. He added, "But this ain't my show". He let out a huge belch and mentioned that the meal was sure good, especially "them prime beef steaks and thet pie, But it don't beat wild buffler."

At Boone's cabin, when a jug was emptied, he'd throw it toward the door and say "Well, there's another dead indin". But I never did witness him and me together draining a whole jug in one sitting. Most of Boone's bottles didn't have any sign of a Federal tax stamp seal. Plus, his plain bottle booze had considerably more chemical taste than the smooth store-bought, factory booze. I doubt anyone would call Boone's juice smooth. I don't know where he got it, but I figured he must have had a friend with a still.

Yep, this was sure different from my first day the year before!

That little jolt of fine corn squeezin' lit me up some, but after Boone quit talking - to himself - as much as to me, I spent as long as I could stay conscious thanking the Lord for this fine day. I knew that I must be the luckiest seventeen-year-old in the whole world. In fact, I felt like I was already in Heaven, right here on the Little Hound Creek. I prayed that the Lord would watch over me and keep me from doing anything to disappoint these fine people who cared about me and had treated me so well. And I prayed to God to not forget my Mom, Pop, sister, Gyp, and the cat, either.

The heavy, freshly washed, old wool blankets weighed me down and gave me a sense of security and peace. Boone's snoring was deep and rhythmic - maybe a bit like a sonic massage. I was soon in deep slumber.

## THE WORK BEGINS

"Drop your cock and grab your socks, it's daylight in the swamp. Aw hell, it's time to hit her, Sprout," was the next thing I heard as Boone drew himself up to a sitting position, then swung his legs off the bed.

I jumped up, pulled on my pants, and was brushing my teeth as I struggled into my shirt. No need to comb my hair, as the hat would cover that mess - I had a flat top crew cut anyway.

Boone told me he never saw anyone brush their teeth before eating, but I told him it kept me from forgetting to do the job amidst the rush to work. We were both out the door in less than five minutes. I grabbed the clean bucket that was sitting on the porch of the cook house and headed to the barn to milk Sara, the Guernsey. Like everry milk cow I'd ever seen, she had beautiful brown eyes. The cats were lined up in anticipation of their shots of warm milk. It seemed like their morning and evening shots of milk were like starting fluid for them - the same as coffee is for most people. But you can never know for sure what's on a cat's mind or what it might do next. I'm not sure a cat knows what's coming next either.

We had the usual big breakfast, fried eggs, biscuits and gravy, sausage, and plenty of toast, butter, and jam, all washed down with coffee. Daylight was breaking as we went out to the porch to pick our teeth, stretch and belch. It was an absolutely beautiful morning.

Peck told me to take Ruben, a son of Goldie and one of my favorite riding geldings, and gather up the other dozen or so saddle horses from across the creek. He said we would go to the dipping vat section to look over the bunch of cattle being held there, while Stan and Boone rode the big field. If I noticed anything amiss - meaning limpers, any animal with a wire cut, or most anything else out of the ordinary, I was to tell Stan. We'd bunch the stock later for the trip to Elkhorn the following day.

It was a great day. We found three sets of cows and calves that would need to stay behind for one reason or another - they were late-birthed calves as I recall, but the main bunch of over three hundred head of Hereford cows with calves would be okay to make the move. A large part of the ranch herd was still at the Whitmore place, so that meant more time in the saddle bringing them to Hound Creek after the first bunch was put on the summer range. I was hoping, even expecting, that I could take part in all of the drives.

After a huge breakfast the next morning we picked up large sacks of lunch goodies and as we saddled the horses, Stan handed me his old 30 U.S. lever action carbine in 30/40 Craig ... in case we ran into a bear.

Peck put his Winchester lever action 25/35 in its scabbard and tied it, butt backward on his saddle, so I tied Stan's carbine the same way.

We quickly gathered the calves to be branded. Branding seemed a cruel treatment for those innocent young animals, and they sure did bawl when the red hot iron seared through their hair and burned well into their hide, but it was necessary for each rancher to mark his stock to avoid either accidental or intentional claims of possession by others. We didn't have but only half a dozen or so to do and the work was finished in about an hour.

The late-born calves had to be branded, so Stan got the irons hot.

As we released each of the kicking, bawling calves I said out loud that I wondered how much it hurt.

Boone offered that it didn't hurt at all. I asked how that could be.

"Jest wear gloves and keep your own hide away from the hot iron and it won't hurt a bit," he explained with a grin.

The next day we four "men" and the two dogs, Pooch and Patch, were off with the cattle, headed for the mountain summer range. The first eighteen miles or so were along the county road which was fenced on both sides, making for easy trailing. We let the cattle walk along slowly to minimize stress and weight loss, giving them plenty of time to drink water at every opportunity. Peck and Stan always treated their cattle with tender respect. We passed Siebens, the neighbor's huge lamb-ing shed, and buildings. Our route took us through a gate and onto the open mountain range. There, without fences, the trailing was more of a chore, but the dogs knew their business keeping the herd together and we made good progress. A couple of miles off the main road was a nice meadow with a cold, clear creek, so we stopped and set up for the night.

We hobbled the horses, Boone made a small fire and we placed our saddles and blankets close enough for some light, but a safe distance away to avoid singeing ourselves or our sleeping rolls. As soon as the sun dropped below the horizon, it got right chilly. Snow drifts still occupied the swales and low places. Boone rattled on about his activities during the century before, focusing on him and his brothers getting the last she-wolf and her litter not far from his cabin in Squaw Hollow. He laughed that nowadays we didn't have to worry too much about getting scalped by "Indins" in our sleep. Of course, he mentioned killing some Indians - but not nearly enough, he never failed to add - which gave him particular satisfaction. Last I remember, he was still droning on when I fell off to a night of shallow sleep.

With the large bunch of cattle so near, I woke up many times that night. I was feeling the cold and halfway expecting - even hoping for a bear. The .30 U.S. was lying on the ground right next to me. But no bruins visited us or the stock. I heard a coyote yapping once - it sounded like a whole pack of them - but the ranch dogs did not respond. I wasn't sure I ever really slept that night, but this was cowboying as I had dreamed it would be, and that was for sure. I figured this is what heaven must, or should, be like.

Just at daylight, Boone had the coffee water boiling, spooned in plenty of grounds and after a few minutes, he poured cold water into the can to settle the coffee grounds. The brew smelled and tasted good. It was starting fluid for the new day for all of us. He seared some bacon and offered it along with bread. We sopped up the bacon grease with the bread and we were soon saddling up. Things were going so well, Peck decided he'd ride on back to the Little Hound Creek, then come up with the Jeep in two or three days.

Dogs, cattle, men, and horses all seemed invigorated, with moods elevating in synchrony with the altitude of the terrane. Just being in the cool clear air of the mountains could do that. I felt like I was living a wonderful dream.

We had the herd in what was to be their summer pasture an hour before dark. The snow cover was much heavier the higher we traveled. Some drifts around the cabin were several feet high.

The cabin was dank and smelly after sitting vacant, except for the resident rats, through the winter, so as Stan fried meat and spuds for dinner, I swept up and partially cleaned the old log shelter. I figured I'd rather sleep outside than in that rodent-dominated housing project, but then there were the bears to consider. The dogs usually opted to stay outdoors.

Elkhorn still had plenty of snow, but it was disappearing fast.

For the next three days, Stan and I rode fence lines, repairing more than a dozen areas that had been torn up by elk. I became familiar with and appreciative of wire pliers. Boone worked around the barn and corral, but I didn't notice any changes or improvements from his days of "labor".

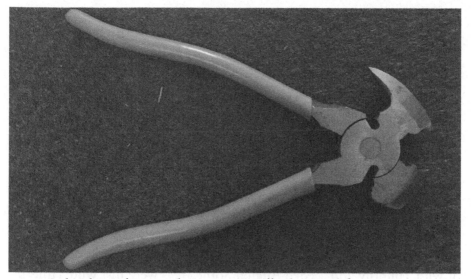

A dandy tool, wire pliers are specially designed for repairing barbed wire fences.

Suddenly, there was new green growth pushing up through the bare ground in almost every place I looked.

Peck arrived in mid-afternoon with food and supplies. He planned for Stan and me to ride back in the jeep with him to Hound Creek. After that, we still had cattle to move up from the Whitmore Place and a string of horses to take to Elkhorn.

Moving horses is far different from moving cattle. It is faster, more exciting, and a whole lot more fun. Cattle are trailed as slowly as possible but horses go on a trot or a run, which is a lot more interesting for a teenage wannabe cowboy. The Staunton Ranch Company had about 90 head of saddle horses and around 40 draft horses, plus "the wild bunch" of young, unbroken horses. For moving longer distances, the two types of equines were moved separately as the big, powerful, workhorses just couldn't keep pace with the quarter horse riding stock. The workhorses were usually kept near the hay fields, anyway, so normally they didn't make the trip to Elkhorn. The heavier saddle horses like Goldie and a big palomino gelding named Banker could pull in harnesses when needed for snaking lodgepole pine out of timber, pulling a wagon, and such-like chores.

The next two weeks were spent moving cattle and horses to the summer range. On occasion, I was plenty tired on the backside, but I truly loved the activity. I was getting so I could drop a loop over a running cow, but I never did get good at throwing the rope very far. Riding Goldie was a huge advantage in working cattle and that mature mare gave me confidence and lined me up to make dropping my loop easy. We saw plenty of mule deer, bear signs, the occasional elk, and several types of smaller wild game, adding to the wonder of it all for me. Groundhogs, or whistle pigs, dutifully alerted the area to our presence. Groundhogs were not as numerous here as they were at Hound Creek. A couple of times we saw some mountain goats way off in the distance. Boone called them "white bufflers". Boone referred to bison as bufflers, too.

By late June we were back to cutting hay. Some fields were a mixture of wild Timothy and seeded Alfalfa. Some areas were just wild Timothy, which we cut and bailed separately for the horses. The fields hadn't needed seeding for several years but they were still producing plenty of hay. Depending on the rain and weather, we expected to get multiple cuttings - up to three - each summer season.

## A RUNAWAY TEAM.

The two fast rake teams at Hound Creek were mine to use and care for. I preferred Pete and Milly. I could ride Milly like a saddle horse with the harness on, but Pete was too twitchy. The other fast team was Boots and Freddie. Boots would suffer a person to use her like a saddle horse, too, but not Freddie. Stan was good with seeing the nature of an individual horse and training the animal to live up to its best potential which included pairing it with a suitable teammate.

The dump rake was a rig with rapier-like tines to pick up hay .. and occasionally snakes. Gunny sacks (nose bags) over the horses' noses reduced fly molestation, which varied from mere irritation to times when huge mobs of insects drove the horses nearly wild.

One hot day in mid-July, Milly was in heat and she kept trying to kick across the tongue of the rake to get at poor old Pete, who as a gelding couldn't service her. She got ornery that way when she came into heat, or her period - kind of like some women, I was beginning to learn. That day she was really cranky. Milly was hooked up on the right side of the team. About mid-afternoon, she managed to kick her left hind leg over the tongue and after a brief struggle, that fine mare fell down. Her hung-up leg hit Pete's hind legs and badly buggered him. He lunged and tried to run. The whites of his eyes were outstanding - real snaky looking, he was. Pete would lunge and Milly, in a panic, would whinney and get dragged. When Pete felt her hoof, he would lunge and go again. I was afraid that the beautiful mare was going to get hurt. When I finally got Pete stopped by pulling back hard on the lines and softly talking to him, Milly continued to struggle, trying to get back on her feet. That mare was, by then, panicked big time and her hysterical action kept Pete wild and ready to plunge ahead.

Me behind Pete and Milly wearing nose bags and pulling the dump rake.

Worried about Milly, I committed the teamster's cardinal sin. *I did not unhook the tug lines as soon as I got off the rig.*

I jumped off the rake seat and walked around to get Pete by the bridle, talking to him soothingly all the time, but as I came along to grab her leather, Milly let out a squeal and lurched to her feet. She came up with all her legs on the correct side of the rake tongue, but she staggered and lunged to break free of the rig. That sent Pete into a panic and the two of them took off. As the rig came my way I dodged away from the deadly rake teeth, but the right wheel caught me and knocked me down. The team was running wild and panicked across the freshly cut field.

They came to a small ditch and the rake went up on one wheel. The tongue and double tree both split, leaving the rake akilter and free of the horses, near a ditch with the single trees noisily banging on the heels of the runaway team, producing a full-out panic in the horses.

They ran like a seriously spooked dog with a tin can tied to its tail.

It was an awful wreck! I was scared to death that the beautiful team was going to get seriously hurt or killed. If either one stumbled or stepped into a soft spot they would probably both go down, and likely one or both could end up with a broken leg or worse. They were a quarter mile away from me in what seemed like no time.

Stan was running the motorized bull rake when he noticed the runaway team. He dumped his load of bunched hay, raised the basket, and made for the team. As the machine loomed up over a rise at full speed, Stan steered for the upended rake, then he swerved toward me when he spotted me running toward the rig. When he got to me, he told me to get in the driver's seat as he climbed onto the frame behind me. He told me to drive to cut the team off as they went around the base of a big hill and to maneuver the machine so I was in front of them. And he barked that I should keep the rake head ratcheted full up.

The horses did not leave the freshly cut stubble but were running at the edge of the long grass. They were still in full panic and at their top speed after about three minutes of sheer terror. I thought I could hear the tug chains clattering along with the single trees as the horses galloped away.

It seemed to take half of forever, but I got the bull rake maneuvered into position, then began to slow down, as Stan told me to do. The wild team did not try to avoid the bull rake. When Pete and Milly were close enough, Stan jumped off the back of the bull rake and got hold of both bridles - and he was able to hang on! They drug him along between them for about fifty yards or so before he could slow them enough to regain his footing and get them stopped. He was talking soothingly to them all the time.

Stan's face was as red as a beet and mine must have been even more so. He kept calmly talking to the horses. I killed the engine and walked over to inspect Milly. The hide on the inside of her left leg was torn up some, but it was mostly just abrasion like what a kid gets when he falls down and skins his knee. A few applications of bag balm and in a week or less she would be fine.

"I know what you did wrong - do you?" Stan asked. He was really upset.

"Yes. I left the rig without immediately unhooking the tugs," was my reply.

"Well, never means never, and you should never forget that, I was thinking you might be speared on some rake tines, or lying bunched up next to the rake tongue. I'm right glad to see you're not hurt", he told me.

Stan told me to drive the bull rake back to the stacker and start pushing more hay, while he rode Milly back and tied the team to the buckboard where they would stay until quitting time. Milly's doctoring could wait until evening. The haying work went on.

At the end of the day, I rode back to the headquarters with the stacker team driver, Old Sully, on the buckboard, with Pete and Milly following behind. Not much was said by the driver or me. Stan drove the bull rake to the shop for routine servicing. Everybody's silence and my dreading of what was bound to come were killing me.

My fowl-up was due to neglect in the face of trouble and I figured my error in judgment resulted in far more serious damage and loss of working time than the worst of Eddie's wrecks and damage to equipment.

Man or boy, I was feeling really low. I had let my team run away. I'd lost 'em. The rig was torn up pretty badly - it was practically destroyed. I felt lucky the horses weren't seriously injured. Nevertheless, I expected to be fired and sent back to the scorched desert. Nobody said a word to me before, during, or after supper. Very few words were uttered by anyone as we ate. It seemed like we were at a funeral or a wake. Vera and the cook looked pitiful so that pretty well confirmed to me that I was going to be canned. And I knew I deserved it.

I had no appetite and ate very little. As I got up with my head hanging down to leave the table, Peck, who must have been reading my emotions, said he reckoned it would take a couple of evenings of work to get that dump rake back in working condition, but for now, I was to go get the spare rake ready. The ranch had at least one spare of almost every piece of critical equipment. I should rub some Bagbalm on Millie's injuries and give her and Pete some extra grain and some kind words.

Peck told me the spare rake was over by the shop and I should take Boots and Freddie to move it to the shop yard to check over, then take it up to the big field in the morning. He said we'd give Pete and Milly a day off.

So, I wasn't fired, at least for the time being. I felt queasy in my heart, but what a relief it was! I had to bite my lip to keep tears from coming.

The spare rake was in fine shape - ready to use, so I asked Stan if I could take Boots and Freddie and the buckboard up to load the broken double tree, find the single trees, and survey any other damage to the rake. He said that would be a good idea and told me to go on up to the field. As I drove up the hill I thanked God for the way this disaster had not turned out as bad as it might have. I was still crossing my fingers in the hope that I had not lost my job ... and Montana. A lone ante-lope buck stood near the gate at the top of the hill, just staring at me. It seemed like the whole world was staring at me. I felt pretty lonely, stupid, and unworthy.

The oak double tree was ruined beyond use, except for firewood, of course, but I found both oak single trees and they were not damaged. After banging on the heels of the horses, the chain tugs came loose from the single tree hooks, and the single trees were left behind. The noise from the terminal chain links on the tugs kept the horses spooked, but they hadn't buggered the horses as badly as the wooden single trees had done.

When I got back to the headquarters I went to the corral and petted and talked with Pete and Milly, apologizing for my stupid mistake. They seemed to accept my heartfelt mea culpa .... or so I told myself.

Stan was working at the shop. He had drug out one of the larger lodge pole pines for a replacement rake tongue and a piece of oak hard-wood lumber to make a new double tree and told me we'd take them and some tools up to the field the next evening and repair the busted dump rake where it was. Then it would be brought back to headquarters and serve as the spare. After supper the following day we had it all back together in a couple of hours.

It had been quite a day. I hit my bunk completely drained but woke up several times from nightmares that had me dropping the lines and the team taking off with me still on the rake, grasping for the lines in front of the rapier-like rake teeth. I was never fearful that I might be hurt, just scared of what damage my neglect might wind up causing. I did not rest well. I might not have actually slept at all that night.

Breakfast was the usual one .... everybody stuffed as much good, high-calorie food down their necks as their bellies could accommodate and it was back up to the big hay field. Table talk was normal and nobody mentioned my accident, which was a relief to me. And, what was even more surprising to me, I didn't feel particularly shunned by anybody.

## THE SEASON OF SNAKES

Rattlesnakes were especially plentiful that summer. I removed at least a couple dozen buzztails from the rake tines in July alone and kept most of the rattles. I encountered a good number of Moccasin Backs ( the local variety of the western diamondback rattler *Crotalus atrox*) under the shocks of oats in August, too. As we pitchforked the shocks into the nearby wagon, the buzz tails were in the shocks to catch rodents and they would tune up as they coiled prior to trying to make their escape. Two of those did escape, but I killed the rest.

The hog yard at Little Hound Creek

Peck kept a sow pig or two to raise enough pork for the ranch. Usually, they had a few surplus hogs which they traded off to neighbors for most anything but mutton or lamb, as Peck, Stan and most other cowmen disdained sheep in any form. A fellow who raised mostly wheat down close to Cascade had a big boar hog that he would loan to those in need of breeding service. Usually, he swapped the boar's activity for beef or whatever else he could use. It was not a "sharp-pencil" swap, it was just friends and neighbors mutually benefitting from little exchanges like that.

I always liked watching hogs eat. It's a scene of sheer, unmitigated delight for them - and for me, too.

Hound Creek hogs were well-fed and gained weight fast.

About a week after borrowing that neighbor's boar hog to service our sow, it was time to return the stud pig. When I picked him up, the neighbor's daughter had helped load the hog. She was a very friendly, pretty gal about my age and I'd been thinking about her and her beautiful long, brown hair and big brown eyes a lot. I was attracted to her, the only girl I'd seen up close since May, but I would have picked her unknown out of a group. She was that nice looking! Her soft brown eyes matched her light brown hair and wonderful soft appearing, inviting lips. So I decided to string a bunch of rattles together and give them to her for a necklace. It would be a pretty neat gift, I thought, but when I presented her the unique, hand-made neckpiece, instead of me getting a hug and a kiss, her smile faded to a frown, and she took a step back and shook her head. I sure didn't expect that reaction!

Her reaction to my rattlesnake - or snake rattle - necklace dashed any dreams I might have had for a date. I, along with the wonderful, one-of-a-kind, homemade neck piece had been summarily rejected. Oh well, there were more productive things to do than chasing a lovely young lady who lived thirty-five miles away. But she was cute ... and her

Daddy had a pretty nice ranch, with no sons to take it over. So much for that dream - it was dashed before it got too strong a grip on me.

The rejected necklace from the summer of 1959. I still have it.

## A LETTER FOR BOONE

One Sunday in July 1959 the haying was going well and at breakfast, Peck announced that the entire crew would get the day off. This was a rare event and came as a complete surprise to everyone. This was my second summer working for the Staunton Ranch Company and I was seventeen years old.

Immediately I began planning what I would do that fine, sunny, nearly windless day. I had it in mind to saddle Ruben and go down Hound Creek as far as possible, with a .22 rifle for groundhogs and a fishing pole for producing a lunch of native Rainbow trout. I would look for shed antlers and Indian arrowheads. The day was nearly cloudless with only gentle thermal breezes as it warmed up. It would be the perfect day to make that trip. My spirit was salivating in anticipation of an adventure aboard Ruben. I'd ride to the top of any high points to search for arrowheads. Who knows what wonderful things I might find? I began most of my trips in similar enthusiastic anticipation.

As everyone was rising to depart the cook house, Peck asked me to stay back, so I did. I wondered what the old man might come up with. He showed me a handwritten envelope with Boone Austin's name on it. It was addressed to him at Little Hound Creek. Peck told me he had no ideas about the letter, or its writer, as he believed all of Boone's kin had long since been done in by Indin's, or old age. But as this was such an unexpected and strange situation, he would see to it that Boone got the letter as soon as practical. The return address was that of Hanna Austin in Harlowtown, Montana. The handwriting was wonderfully controlled and graceful, unlike my own scribble-scratching.

"Jake, would you mind taking the jeep and delivering the letter to Boone up to Elk Horn today? And you'd better carry my 25/35 along in case you run into that bear Boone's been yammering about. That offer of the rifle was irresistible bait for me. Peck said he had to prepare for a meeting with the ranch's accountant next week, or he would do the trip himself.

Coming on the heels of my disastrous run-away team, this was surprising, but it seemed to mean that I was held in at least a little respect and trust.

I was stunned. Gone were my dreams of spending the day in the wild country down the creek with Reuben, maybe finding shed deer antlers or even a buffalo carcass, cooking fresh-caught rainbow trout on a stick, and maybe making some extra money shooting groundhogs. Poof. Gone. Rats! But Peck's request trumped all else, in my view.

The trip down the creek was a serious draw for me, but after a split moment's consideration of Peck's request for making a trip to Elk Horn with the rifle - that was potentially even better - and maybe the bear would present itself! Plus, I could not deny Peck anything he requested, and I enjoyed spending time with Boone. His stories, though often repeated, were ongoing and always fascinating to me.

"Well, sure Peck, I'd be happy to do that. Is there anything else to take to him?"

Peck said the cook already had a couple of boxes of groceries, including two pies and some bags of cookies that I should resist sampling until Boone offered me some.

Peck had me load some sacks of oats and a half dozen blocks of salt in the back of the jeep pickup to keep as spare supplies if not needed that summer. He and my Uncle Stan always operated that way - getting several things done at the same time, for little or no extra effort or expense. Never making a partial load became my way of life, too, especially years later when making aircraft flights to the lodge on Trail Creek.

So less than a half hour later and still just shortly after sunup, I was driving up the county road, with the floor and shotgun seat full of supplies for Boone, and the rifle wedged in for quick access if an opportunity came. I really liked that octagon-barreled carbine. The bluing was almost completely worn off, but the weapon had received good care for many decades. I treated it as if it was a treasure of my own.

It was a perfectly beautiful, sunny day in the Big Sky country and my spirit matched the weather. Montana always smells so good to me with grass, trees, horses and all mixed in with fresh cow and horse poop.

As I passed the Sieben's lambing sheds some fellows were cleaning up and working on machinery. I waved to a couple of familiar faces I'd seen the summer before when we were thrashing oats. They gave me a hearty wave back. I was never good at remembering names.

As the road got steeper and the timber grew thicker I kept on high alert for a bear. Now THAT would make the day even more perfect - seeing - then maybe shooting and skinning a bruin!

I drove by two families of Fool Hens (*Falcipennis canadensis*) walking along the road and silently wondered what their false penis would look like - or why they were called that. As I had no .22 rifle, the grouse did not get shot for the pot. I ruminated on the fact that I could probably get one or two with a rock or the short piece of chain I carried for just that purpose, but the chain was in my saddle bag back in the tack room in the barn. So I just drove on.

The new grass in the high mountain meadows smelled good enough for even me to eat. No wonder the cattle did so well on their summer range!

The jeep topped over the ridge and began the gentle descent to the old log cabin and barn at Elk Horn. Boone had heard me coming and had a brew of coffee on the pot belly stove, ready to pour.

"Well, Sprout, it's a surprise to see you behind the wheel. Usually, Peck brings me my groceries and stuff," Boone said in his raspy voice.

Boone's preferred type of personal poison.

The old Indin fighter pawed through the bags, first to find his smoking tobacco and papers. He preferred Duke's Mixture but would use whatever he could find. He lifted out a bag of Duke's blend and some packages of Top Fine Gummed Cigarette Papers and proceeded to roll a smoke right away. Modern life had come to this part of the mountains and luxuries such as tobacco were now expected. He offered, so I made a clumsy attempt at rolling a smoke. I needed to learn that I reckoned, but I never liked the taste or smell of cigarette smoke.

Usually, Peck or the cook would toss in a Western or detective magazine or sometimes a National Geographic. This time I had added some comic books and one "man's" magazine from the bunkhouse. That magazine had a full-page picture of a very attractive tall woman standing in a see-through nightie that revealed a dark, mysterious bushy patch below her belly button. I thought about it, and she looked nice.

As Boone stored his groceries in their proper places, I noticed fresh rat pellets on the floor and some on a chest-high shelf. I realized that he wasn't living completely alone up at the summer camp.

I offered to help, but Boone told me he had to place his supplies just right - so he could find them later.

I took my cup outside where the air smelled fresh, unlike the stale disgusting odor of the old log shelter.

As I finished up my first cup, Boone came out to sit next to me. Before he launched into one of his long old-timer stories, I handed him the letter. It was addressed to *Boone Austin, Little Hound Creek Ranch, Cascade, Montana.*

Boone squinted hard and declared "Well, Glory be, must be from little Hanna's girl !"

As Boone figured it, "Little Hanna" was a shirt-tail niece and must be the daughter of one of his brother's daughter's daughters - or something like that.

"Heh, heh," he marveled. "Didn't think I had any blood still alive in the world, but I shoulda knowed better, as us Austins is all made tough."

Boone handed the short page of handwritten script to me and asked me to read it out loud, to make sure he had it right. He was making a smoke again and offered me the makin's, but one smoke was more than enough for me. The tobacco was harsh, but I puffed on it anyway, more to satisfy Boone than myself.

It read: *Dear great uncle Boone. I am here, living in Harlowtown, in Wheatland County, on the Mussleshell River. Just south of Judith Gap. One of Daddy's old acquaintances told me he heard you were alive and living in the Little Belt Mountains, maybe on Little Hound Creek. That old man, Waller was his name, said I should try to see you sometime.*

*It would be nice to see you and it would be nice for you to come to see me here in the Judith Basin where I was told you used to come to hunt some of the last wild buffalo in Montana.*

*I will cook up a big meal, with apple pie, and you can stay in the house here if you can come.*

*Well, Uncle Boone, if this letter finds you, it would be so nice to get together.*

*Sincerely,*

*Hanna Austin*

Wow! That was like a bolt from the blue! Boone was excited, but he did his best to not show his feelings. He leaned back and nearly fell off the stump he was sitting on. Then he straightened up and drew deep on his cigarette. Obviously, he was thinking deeply.

"Sprout", he told me, "everything's in fine shape here. No pink eye, salt's all out, fences fixed, and the bear ain't showed himself for quite a spell. I think it would be all right for me to go out with you and then go visit my long-lost niece. It'd only take a couple of days, then I could come right back. The cattle and the rats won't miss me much."

I told Boone that sounded like a fair idea to me and he drew himself up, went back inside the old cabin, and began to rattle around, getting his stuff ready to travel. He left one saddle horse in the big corral that had plenty of grass still standing and he threw in a chunk of Timothy hay. The trickle from the creek branch kept the water tank full and all should hold fine, and look about the same when he came back, he reckoned.

The cooler box was built over a small stream which kept the eggs and perishables from spoiling. It was all pretty much self-sustaining. But, just in case, we each ate a big piece of the pie - a whole quarter of a pie, apiece, and he took one of the bags of cookies to feast on as we traveled.

And we were off to the ranch headquarters on Little Hound Creek - Boone with his dirty old sleeping bag and of course, his smokes and chewin' tobaccy.

The day remained sunny and warm, making our ninety-minute drive to Little Hound Creek really enjoyable. Better still, Boone ranted on and on about how he, as a young boy, went a time or two to the Judith Basin to get some "buffler" meat, but even then bufflers and all the big game was getting more and more scarce. He said he doubted we'd see any on this trip. His enthusiasm grew with every word. I was getting excited, too. I tried to stay alert for a bear, but Boone's talking distracted me. We saw some mule deer as we started down the hill toward Siebens and then a big bunch of sixty or so Pronghorns between the sheep outfit and the home place.

We pulled into the yard shortly after noon, and Boone got out at the cookhouse to thank the old cook for her pastries and magazines. Peck came out and was surprised to see Boone. He said we should all go in and get some lunch.

The two men talked a little, then Boone came to my cabin and told me that Peck gave his approval for Boone to take a few days off to visit his relative, but he needed to go back up to Squaw Hollow to get some of his stuff for the trip. He said Peck suggested he ask me to take him up in the jeep, which I was more than happy to do

The one-lane track up the creek was not too difficult to drive, as there had been little rain for the past two weeks. It took less than an hour to get to his old log squatters' shack. When I shut down the engine, his cat, named Mike, named for an older brother who was killed and mutilated by Blackfeet, came out from under the log cabin and sidled up to Boone's leg. He picked up the cat which licked his face and pulled a piece of dried venison out of his pocket for the feline, which immediately started up its purr motor.

We were only a little over half an hour at Boone's old squatter's shack before we drove back down the creek.

Boone dumping out a pan of stale water he'd left sitting since going up to Elk Horn in May. He stood a bit over six feet tall and was not too bent or bad off for his close to ninety years of living in the wilds of Montana.

I don't know how old Boone's cabin was, but it was warm and didn't leak when it rained. He said that he and one of his brothers built it a long time back.

Peck told us the plan was that we would head out the next morning for Harlowtown, with a couple of small pieces of haying equipment to drop off in Cascade for repair. Peck mentioned that I should do the driving and we should go to the "Falls" (Great Falls) then head south to Armington Junction where just past the town I should take the right fork of the road to Monarch. We'd be seeing the Judith Basin at its best - in July.

Wow! I was excited. I was going to see some new country - and in the company of old Boone, who hadn't been there for probably fifty years. I knew he'd have a bunch of stories to tell as we drove along.

That evening with Boone already asleep in the bunk next to me, Stan came over and told me to come with him. Peck wanted to talk with me. I pulled my pants and shirt on and followed Stan to Peck and Vera's house.

Peck had been able to reach Hanna by telephone through an old friend of his in Harlowtown, so she would be expecting the two of us sometime the next day.

Peck said that we should plan to stay overnight in Harlowtown to let Boone have time with his niece. If more than one night looked necessary, that would be fine, but I should call the ranch. He told me that Boone probably would not want to drive - and he really shouldn't - he ought to just ride along. He said he wished he could take Boone, but the ranch accountant had set up a meeting a month before. Even Vera, who normally disparaged Boone as "that danged old reprobate" seemed excited for him about this trip.

Peck said when we were ready to come back, which would probably be on Tuesday, I should drive due north to Judith Gap, then turn west to Hebson and Geyser. It was a different route than the one I was to take going to Harlowtown, but faster, and I would see some important places from Montana's recent past, but I should be sure to depart early enough to have good light for the trip. He added that I should stop at Bill's service station in Cascade to pick up a highway map when I dropped off the two pieces of mowing machines to be welded. And I should remember to milk the cow and slop the hogs before I left in the morning. Stan added that I ought to scrape off some of the grime on my face, maybe even take a bath before going on the trip!

Peck offered us each a pull on his bottle of Old Grandad, one hundred-proof whiskey, so we each enjoyed a short snort.

Bathing wasn't handy at the ranch, with no shower and all. Most of the men just went without or splashed a quick handful of creek water on their faces. Me, I hated to scrape off too much of the natural protective crust I wore, but that evening I did wash up with cold water and soap in the hand basin.

Boone snored the night away, and in my excitement about the trip, I don't know if I ever slept at all. I was up and wide awake before the usual time, so I milked the Guernsey early with the barn cats acting a bit miffed as they sat to receive their squirts of milk right from the cow's tit. They would catch some of the squirts right in their mouth, then spend time licking up the spillage on their face and neck. As I squeezed the tits with my face in her flank, the cow's side was warm and smelled good. As I went out the door, I took a can of Right Guard - which Stan used to spray on an orphaned calf so another cow would accept it. I sprayed a little on me, for the big trip. I took a full bucket of milk to the spring house, which I exchanged for a couple of pails of hog slop - which was old milk and scrapings from the cook house plates. The hogs were appreciative, as always, no matter what the hour.

Someone, probably Stan, had left some boot oil and a brush in my little cabin, so I gave my boots a little care. Boone had already done his before he went to bed.

The old cook, Edna, who was Eddie's grandma, had heard the news and told me she heard Eddie might be living on a ranch near Harlowtown, so maybe I could tell him hello for her.

Poor old gal, there was no way this side of the grave I was going to look for Eddie Skelton, the bully I had jerked off his horse, and thoroughly whomped the summer before.

There's nothing that shows more pure gusto than a bunch of hogs at the trough.

So as the rest of the haying crew was getting ready to go up to the big field, Boone and I drove up the road, turned right, and crossed the steel bridge. As we felt the bump off the end of the bridge, we were overcome by the fresh smell of skunk! I'd received some direct shots of skunk spray when I was trapping near home in southern Arizona, and one time while crawling through a culvert with a couple of friends and one irritated skunk, but this was nearly as horrible. Apparently, the skunk darted out from beneath the bridge and got hit by the right front tire, squished, flattened, and killed, then flung up into the wheel well.

"Well, I'll be kill and scalp an Indin," Boone hollered. Get this contraption over to the side of the road. We gotta see if the stinking polecat got inside the engine.

We had to force ourselves to get close to the miasma in the wheel well. As we approached a hissing noise could be heard. Boone said the skunk was really provoked and hissing at us, so he stood back a few feet. As I proceeded cautiously toward the vehicle, with a stick I picked up out of the ditch, I noticed the tire was rapidly going flat! That explained the hissing.

The skunk was flattened and dead, but one of its leg bones had splintered and penetrated the tire in between the treads. The bloody, twisted black and white carcass was hung up on a piece of metal at the top of the wheel well. Likely we were going to get plenty smelly as we changed that tire.

Boone got a stick and after multiple attempts over several minutes, he flipped the mangled mustelid remains into the roadside ditch. The old Indian fighter had a spell of sneezing and severe coughing such as I had never seen before, as I got ready to change the flat tire. I hoped he would be able to make the trip to Harlowtown. His hacking and coughing brought up a wad of sputum that looked like an oyster. Then he shook himself and straightened up to full height and said he was fine.

We had a HI-lift bumper jack, so there was no need for me to get underneath the vehicle, and that no doubt saved me from a worse dose of skunk juice.

I put an old pair of gloves on and tried to keep my clothes from touching the tire as I put it in the back. Boone thanked me for doing the change.

Bill's service station in Cascade.

We smelled that dead skunk all the way down the road, past the Whitmore Place, and the Loy Place, both of which were also owned by the Staunton Ranch Company, and across the bridge to Cascade on the Missouri River ... the stench lingered.

I pulled up to Bill's service station and he came out to greet us, but stopped short, saying "What kinda mayhem have you two young fellers got into so early on a Monday morning? I mean, a skunk and what else?"

We, or rather, mostly Boone, related our recent debacle to Bill who had suggested that while he repaired the tire, I could take his pump sprayer and hit the wheel well with Stoddard Solvent (a de-greaser) to cut the smell as much as possible. Home-canned tomatoes would work better, but none was available. So, as Boone went on with telling about our battle with the dead skunk, I sprayed. Boone told the story truthfully, which convinced me to trust his other stories.

The tube was patched and the spare tire was put in place. Bill kept shaking his head, wondering just how the devil that thigh bone had broke and done such damage. Bill threw another mounted tire in the back, so we'd have two spares in case we got into a fight with a bigger skunk. We could return it when we came by for the repaired pieces of machinery.

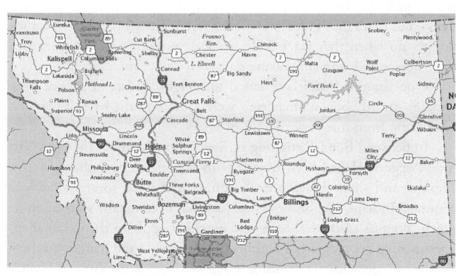

Bill handed me a highway map.

Bill mentioned how unusual and unlucky that skunk bone splintering and poking through the tire was. He'd never seen the like of it! It was so unlucky, maybe that would use up all or most of our bad luck for the trip, but I should be extry careful anyway. Bad luck usually comes in threes he reminded us.

We topped off the fuel tank and drove on toward "the Falls."

As we drove past Ulm, Boone told me that the surrounding country was originally one big ranch owned by an Easterner named William Ulm. For thousands of years before that, "Indins" had driven large herds of buffalo over a cliff, now called *Ulm Pishkun*. He had several comments to make about the "Indins" supposedly never wasting anything, which was a danged pack of black lies, he said. There were several hundred such sites of "Indin" waste in Montana, but this was maybe the biggest one. He said he reckoned them "Red hide niggers" had wasted millions of prime bufflers over the thousands of years. "Just ran 'em up the north side of the butte and had the squaws and kids spook 'em over the cliff on the south side. 'Course most of the meat got wasted, no tellin' how many broke-leg beasts bawled, bellowed, and suffered for days before dying, but that's the "Indin" way - even today. Jest you look at how those savages do when they get a dollar in their pocket, and how they treat their horses and women," Boone said with contempt.

One account I read later stated that eighteen feet of packed bison remains -mostly bones, of course - were located at the base of that cliff. That came from one heck of a lot of bison.

In between Boone's gripping stories, I thought about the term "Red hide Niggers". I had been friends with some Acoma Indians in New Mexico, and some Apaches in Arizona and I liked some of the local Montana Indians, like Broken Nose Joe, that occasionally worked on the ranch. Boone's epithetical term sure wouldn't apply to them, but then I guess people get prejudicial notions in their heads and hang onto them. For sure, some cultural prejudices result from seeing the same bad behavior over and over, so in that sense, the prejudice might be understood, but probably not justified, or so I figured. Then too, prejudice may just be self-preservation - the survival instinct kicking in.

I thought about how Swedes were referred to as "Square Heads," which never bothered me. Like Gram always said, "Stick and stones may break your bones, but words will never harm you - unless you let 'em."

But I also realized that if I had found a brother - or maybe even a stranger - that had been tortured and mutilated with ears and nose cut off, eyes gouged out, with penis and testicles cut off - some or all of which were done while my brother was still alive - I would be thinking about killing every member of the group that had done such torture. That was all in Boone's history. I had read eyewitness accounts of how Apaches would stake an enemy out on an ant hill, cut off his eyelids and urinate on him, then leave him to die that way. I wondered how anybody could ever be that mean to another human being - it is even worse to treat animals cruelly.

Well, I sure hoped I would never be on the receiving side of such an experience, and in the meantime, I would try to avoid unjustified prejudices.

Then again I remembered how so many people professed to not be prejudiced, but actually, just about everyone was prejudiced to some degree, whether they admitted it or not.

Boone said it was too bad we didn't have time to go see the buffalo site, but we had better things to do than poke around old "Indin" garbage.

The day was warm and the skunk essence was still with us, so we left the windows wide open. It's amazing how much stamina that skunk smell has! I wondered what else traveled with the speed of smell. I read someplace that skunk juice could be denatured and cleaned up, then used in women's perfume to give it staying power. I wondered about that.

As we approached "the Falls" Boone pointed off to the northwest and told me that Hill Fifty-seven was over yonder. That was a collection of "Indin" hovels where some of the landless Chippewa, Cree, and Metis Indians lived, along with assorted reservation jumpers. Most families had up and left, but some of the most worthless, lazy ones remained. Some of them worked occasionally as haying crewmen for nearby ranches.

"That's a good place to stay away from, Sprout, drunk or sober," Boone assured me.

I asked Boone where the Falls were. He rattled off, "The original Rainbow Falls that Lewis and Clark discovered in 1805 and was seen by me and my family, was dammed about 1910 when Rainbow Dam was built. The reservoir behind the dam submerged Colter Falls. Volta Dam was built on top of the Great Falls in 1915 and later renamed Ryan Dam. Altogether there were five big waterfalls, where today we see none at all."

That old man had a great memory! He had seen and been part of a lot of history.

It was sometimes difficult for me to think analytically with Boone rattling on as he always did. Maybe so much time spent alone prompted him to talk incessantly when he had an audience - especially an audience as eager, naive, and attentive as I was.

But, I thought, if Columbus got to America in 1492 and Coronado got to New Mexico with horses about fifty years later, the plains Indians only had horses since about 1650 or so. So, most of those massive buffalo stampedes must have taken place while the Indians were still afoot. That made it more understandable to me for them to stampede a bunch of bison over a cliff - when they only had moccasins on their feet, not horses under 'em. And no rifles - just bows and arrows. They just got meat by whatever means they had. It was still an awful waste, but more reprehensible when it happened after the Indians had horses. Seemed like old habits died hard with Indians, same as with some white folks.

Peck had mentioned for me to find excuses, if necessary, to not stop at a liquor store for Boone until we were on the way back. It would be okay for Boone to buy a small bottle to sip and suck on, but not until after our time in Harlowtown, so I skirted around the usual cowboy haunts such as the Mint Bar and Cafe where we sometimes shanghaied drunks to take to work on the haying crews. We drove through Great Falls and got onto the road south to Armington without a stop.

Driving east from Great Falls for about twenty-five miles we traveled through some pretty flat rolling, grassy hills with occasional fenced rectangles of wheat or oats. Boone told me this used to be ideal buffalo country, but the wild bufflers had been all shot off, except for a few that were kept as pets. A short way out of Armington we came to the junction of Highways 87 and 89. I took the right fork toward Monarch. The country grew more interesting with deeper canyons and bigger timber as we got out of the foothills and into another part of the Little Belt Mountains.

We passed through Monarch without making a stop. Traveling south it seemed like every mile or less we'd pass a homesite or little ranch. I didn't like seeing the country so cut up and domesticated. Boone said it made him feel sick to his stomach to see so many people cluttering up and spoiling the good country. Some of 'em even had grass yards to mow!

"Aw, sprout," he told me, "you shoulda seen this piece of the country well back into the century before when it was wild, fulla game, and short of people. 'Stead of shelling out hard cash for something to eat, ya just had to put a grasshopper on a hook to catch a fish or throw a rock at a prairie chicken to make your lunch. If you run into "Indins" you could either avoid 'em or figure a way to kill and scalp 'em. That prime time ain't never comin' back, neither. And look at all the fences and people - they're everywhere!"

To me, it was depressing to hear Boone reminiscing about the good old days. He'd go on for a while, then just remain quiet for a spell - in deep melancholy, I figured. More than once he mentioned that I, Sprout, had been born at least a hundred years too late. I had felt that way for a long time, too,

We summited King's Hill at over eight thousand feet, then the road turned hard west for four or five miles before turning south. Signs told us White Sulphur Springs was just ahead so I drove the extra couple of miles past our turn-off to Harlowtown to get a bite to eat. Signs indicated there were hot springs there and Boone said we just had to take a look at the Sherman Castle, which was an impressive castle made out of granite that was hauled by oxen from the Castle Mountains. Apparently, a guy named Sherman was a rancher who had made it big and wanted to live like a king. He rigged up a hydro-electric plant and sold power to the town, but eventually, he moved off to sunny California. Then his castle was bought by the town and turned into a museum.

Sherman's castle

We pulled up to a small grocery store and got us some simple fixin"s - baloney, a small tin of butter, and biscuits, to kill our craving for food. Baloney was sort of a treat, but Boone told me it was mostly armpits and bungholes ironed out. Otherwise, it would be in wieners - tube steaks, he said. Awful stuff, he snorted, but it would do in a pinch. We washed it all down with some water from the jug of Hound Creek water I had brought. We still had some cookies left, too. Boone said we didn't want to arrive at his niece's in a starved-looking condition. We chewed down our lunch on the road to Harlowtown. With so much wind in the cab due to the open windows, instead of rolling a smoke, Boone was taking a pinch of Copenhagen every now and then. He offered some to me, but it made me feel sick, so I would slyly spit it out as soon as he turned his head.

I counted five road-killed porcupines in as many miles shortly after departing White Sulphur Springs. I wondered if their quills could penetrate a tire.

It was only about sixty miles to our destination, but the sun was sinking low, so we didn't have much time for any side trips, though the country was inviting. We did divert over across the Musselshell River to Two Dot and drove through real slow. There were some old stone and brick buildings, including a long abandoned State Bank building made of brick. I wondered why nobody bought it to live in. There were some ancient log buildings and of course a bar. People, way back when built stuff to last, it seemed. I decided I wouldn't mind living in this area, but Hound Creek was better.

About supper time we came to Harlowtown, which sits surrounded by the Crazy, Little Belt, and Big Snowy Mountains. It was beautiful. We drove past the Graves Hotel which looked like it was made of the same granite that built Sherman's castle.

Boone had me stop at a bar so he could use a telephone to contact his niece. He was licking his lips but resisted ordering a whiskey due to not wanting to smell like booze when, at last, he met his long-lost niece. I was proud of the old fellow - and mildly surprised.

After being all day with the windows open, I could still, but barely, detect the odor of polecat, so I hoped it would not be enough to be picked up by Boone's relatives. I was glad I'd sprayed myself with Stan's Right Guard.

Well, I almost wished we had not eaten the baloney and biscuits. As soon as we walked into Hanna's well-kept little house I could smell supper and freshly baked apple pie. My stomach came alive and began to rumble.

Hanna hugged Boone, which caused him to cringe a bit, then he introduced me, " Hanna this here's Sprout …."

I interrupted and said, "Most people just call me Jake, Miss Hanna."

"Yeah, that's right, this here's Jake, Stan Nason's nephew," Boone said.

Hanna looked to be about in her mid-fifties and did not look at all like Boone, which was lucky for any woman. She was about five feet four inches tall, lean, and weighed maybe a hundred and thirty pounds. She was a handsome woman by any man's estimation. And she was friendly and properly spoken. She had taught grade school for many years. I thought if she was forty years younger I would like to ask her to dance.

Hanna had kept her word. She had thick T-bone steaks, baked potatoes, and salad, then the pie with vanilla ice cream on top.

Both Boone and I looked pretty scruffy having no haircuts or shaves for quite some time. Hanna told us that she used to cut her husband and sons' hair and she would be happy to give us each a trim. I would have enjoyed the barbering, but Boone politely declined for us both.

Neighbors and friends began to come by to visit, as Hanna had put the word out to the little community. Five elderly ladies came and stayed the entire evening. People were really curious about old Boone and all were polite to me, asking me a few questions just to keep me in the conversation. But the collection of old ladies made me weary, especially after a day of driving with so much wind in my face.

One of the older gals, I think her name was Millie, said she was sure Jake would be interested in some of the local Indian stories. Since Harlowtown and the Judith Basin were part of the high plains country, they used to have large herds of buffalo which drew Indians from many tribes, including Sioux, Crow, Blackfeet - which were the worst, Flathead, Gros Ventre (Big bellies), Northern Cheyenne, Nez Perce (pierced nose), Shoshones, and Assiniboine, and probably some more. Some tribes were related and friendly with one another, but most were not.

Millie told us we would probably see plenty of teepee rings on the way north. These were rings of stones used to hold down the perimeter of the old-time teepees. Some dated back over a thousand years, she said. To myself, I wondered how anybody could know that.

The most world-changing event occurred when the Spanish explorers brought horses to the new world. Eventually, enough horses escaped - "or were stolen !"- interrupted one of the ladies - to become available to plains Indians. The introduction of the horse made life a lot easier and led to huge increases in the number of Indians. By the time trappers, then miners, settlers, and homesteaders arrived, the Indians were highly mobile and defensive of their homelands. So there were lots of fights and ongoing wars between whites and Indians. From about 1860 to 1900, there was apt to be trouble anytime whites and Indians met. Two of the most wrinkled old gals, probably in their seventies, but looking much older than Boone, told us that they recalled losing close family members to hostile Indians.

Hanna said that her great uncle Boone, sitting here with us, could probably tell us some first-hand stories of Indian fighting.

Boone was tired after such a long and unusual day, and too many old ladies, so he just said he hated to get started on how many of them Indins he had scalped as a young man. I was relieved that he had not used his usual epithet for Indians.

Some of the old heifers recoiled a bit at Boone's comments, but it was a good thing he said that, because right afterward, the old ladies began, one and two at a time, to head home.

My face got tired of smiling. I fell asleep in my chair.

When I glanced at my Timex, it was already past eleven. Nine o'clock or earlier was my usual bedtime. As her guests began to depart, Hanna said Boone could use the spare bedroom and I could sleep on the couch, if I didn't mind. She was gracious in everything she did, that fine woman.

Having maybe not slept much at all the night before, I was asleep before I closed my eyes and did not wake up until I heard the rattle of pots and pans in the kitchen before six the next morning. Hanna was fixing a working man's breakfast of hash brown spuds, fried eggs, and sausage with a platter of steaks already in the middle of the table.

I ate pretty light, as I had the morning before, figuring we would be sitting on our butts the rest of the day going back to Hound Creek. No need to stuff myself to distention and discomfort if I wasn't going to put in a hard day's work, I figured.

But small-town folk in rural Montana were still basically farm or ranch people and at about seven that morning neighbors began to trickle in, so we were stuck with visiting at least for the morning. I got the impression that some of the visitors just wanted to take a look at Boone.

It seemed to me that Boone was trying to break free of the old ladies when he mentioned that we'd really ought to buy a nice lunch for Hanna down at the Graves Hotel, which only served breakfast and lunch. He was probably planning for us to escape right afterward to get on the road with good daylight for the trip home.

So, as soon as the chattering old ladies began to disperse, Boone, Hanna, and I headed for the Graves before eleven o'clock. Hanna drove her car so we could all ride inside. I was quick to open the door for the others and we sat at the lunch counter. Boone was studying the bar and all the bottles on the shelf, but he resisted ordering a drink.

Prices weren't too high, but we all ordered cheap - just hamburgers and coffee. The food was good. Hanna said she had another pie she would send with us when we left. Boone insisted on paying the bill, so I left a dollar for a tip. There was a showcase full of tourist junk which none of us looked at. I headed to the door and opened it for Hanna and Boone.

The Graves Hotel in Harlowtown

As I was standing on the porch holding the door open, I heard something behind me to my left and started to turn to see it, when something hit me really hard on the left side of my head. Suddenly I saw stars, they seemed like Fourth of July sparklers in my head. I had no idea what happened, but I looked up from the porch to see Boone standing over me hollering at a couple of angry-looking young men.

"Ya sucker punched him, but by God, I'm not a-gonna see you kick him when he's down."

Hanna was right next to Boone, ready to do whatever was necessary. Then she went to somebody's pickup parked in front and came back with a long-handled shovel which she gave to Boone, in case he needed it. Hanna had been around violence before it seemed.

My head cleared slowly and I realized there were two fellows a couple of years older than me hollering at Boone, and one of them looked like Eddie Skelton, but wasn't him. Nothing made sense. I was woozy and my legs were soft as mush.

By sheer dumb luck, the local sheriff came cruising by and upon seeing the altercation, came up on the porch. He said, "I know you damned trouble-makers. You Skeletons are all alike - now you just stand there and shut up, until I check this fellow. As the two young men started to leave, the sheriff hollered "I said to stand there and be quiet until I tell you to do otherwise." So the sheriff knew these two already.

Boone and the sheriff helped me get to my feet. My vision was clearing and my legs were getting more steady, but I could feel my left cheek already swelling up.

The one that looked like Eddie started yelling that I had broken his cousin's ribs and stomped him while he was down the year before and he was just setting things right.

"And I told you twice to shut up! And keep shut up until I get this sorted out. Next time it'll be handcuffs for you, two" the sheriff warned.

For sure I was developing a heck of a shiner, but I'd survived plenty of black eyes before. I wondered how those guys could have recognized me.

Boone told the sheriff he didn't know anything about me breaking ribs on anybody, but I knew he had heard the story. He was covering for me.

The sheriff asked me about breaking ribs last year. I said yes, I had a fight with Eddie Skelton who was three years older than me and much bigger. I got tired of him trying to bully me, so I jerked him off his horse and kicked him in the ribs a few times. After that, he got canned by the Staunton Ranch Company and I heard he went to Reform School.

The sheriff said he thought anybody who sucker punches a peaceful younger fellow like me, ought to be put in jail.

Now Eddie's two cousins got to hollering and said they were going to call their Dad and get a lawyer.

The sheriff pulled out his handcuffs and asked if he needed to use them - then without another word, he put one bracelet on each, so the two were unable to separate. The one that hit me said he thought his right hand was broken, and it did look pretty swollen up. The sheriff wasn't too gentle putting the cuff on that hand, as the guy winced and moaned. He snapped the other cuff on the second guy's right hand too, which made it difficult for them to move around. He told them to get in the back of his car, as they were going to sit in his jail for a spell.

This all took place in probably less than five minutes. I felt a little sick to my stomach, which usually means I have a broken bone. I guessed it must be my left cheekbone - the zygomatic arch.

So after the sheriff wrote down everybody's name and address he said we could go. He gave me his business card. He drove the Skeltons off to jail.

Hanna insisted that she tend my injury, but it was only to use a damp washcloth to soothe my cheek a little. I wasn't cut and there was no blood. Then she took a washcloth (we called them washrags in those days) which she folded and placed around some ice cubs. She told me to hold it to my cheek to minimize bruising and swelling. I think my treatment helped her more than it did me, but it was nice of her to do it. Boone said we ought to hit the road if I felt like it, which I certainly did.

So we loaded into the jeep and took the road north to Judith Gap. I drove with the ice bag tied to my head with Boone's handkerchief until I got a "country headache" - similar to the type one gets from drinking very cold water too fast, so I laid the makeshift ice bag on the seat.

We drove a bit east of the little town of Utica and after my surprise altercation in Harlowtown, I was reminded of one of my favorite Charlie Russel paintings.

*In Without Knocking* by Charlie Russel

As I turned my head to observe something on the right, Boone noticed my swollen left cheek and commented that I wasn't looking too symmetrical just then. I noticed my eye slit on the left side was getting narrower. The swelling was getting worse.

The country was mostly natural rolling grassland, interrupted by fenced-off farmed patches of grain or alfalfa. The Snowy and Belt Mountains were visible on the East and West sides. My companion kept musing about how there should be herds of bufflers, 'stead of so many ticky-tacky little farms and stuff.

In what used to be the town of Buffalo, we passed a deserted bank building, some long-neglected ranch buildings, and an old grain silo. There was nothing much left of that place, but somebody's memories.

As we drove along, Boone said we should pull over, then go look at what was left of some teepee rings.

It wasn't much, just a bunch of medium-sized rocks in a circle, but it looked to be man-made.

Remains of an old Teepee ring.

We drove to Hobson, saw more old wooden grain elevators, crossed the Musselshell River, and came to Mocassin. There was a pretty impressive building sitting deserted. I thought it would make a fine, big home, but it looked like nobody cared for it. I saw fine stands of lodgepole pine in the hills, which might have drawn Indians back in the old days. We used that sort of pole for our bull rake and stacker head teeth.

Down the road a few miles we came to Windham which didn't show us much - just a few abandoned wooden buildings and more buffalo country without any buffalo. But we did see a few Pronghorns, or "goats" as Boone called them.

On north a few miles we came to Stanford which according to a road sign, started out as a station on the Fort Benton-Billings stage route. It served as a meeting place for cowboys from the Judith Basin Pool and other cattle companies who grazed cattle on the rich Judith Basin grasses before homesteaders and sheepmen arrived. Now it was just another little rural town with false-front stores lining the single street. There were plenty of alfalfa stacks, most were loose-stacked hay, with a few bale stacks.

The day was hot, probably in the nineties as we toured north, enjoying the fresh smells of Montana grasses, sedges, and what-not. Up the road about three miles, we saw dark-colored smoke. When we got to the site it appeared that a stack of loose hay had caught fire and burned quickly. There were some pickup trucks and men watching what was left of the fire. Boone told me it was probably from spontaneous combustion which is caused by damp hay being put up before being properly dried out. It generates heat in the stack and - poof, it busts into flame. Boone said nobody ever was able to put out a stack fire caused naturally like that because they seem to explode when they go off.

We saw no skunks that day, but we did see several porcupines flattened out on the blacktop pavement. I avoided running over the carcasses.

As one might expect, near the little town of Geyser, there were some small mud geysers, which I reckoned must be somehow part of the same underground thermal system that ran north from Yellowstone Park. A sign along the road stated that this was an overnight stop on the Great Falls-Lewistown stage route. In the 1800s the availability of homestead land drew many people from Finland, the descendants of whom still inhabit the area. I noticed mailboxes with Finnish-sounding names on them. I also noticed an occasional faint whiff of skunk which was still coming from the wheel well. What staying power!

The town of Raynesford was named for some old-timer, Boone reckoned. "A whole lot of people like to put their name on a place, but they just die, rot, and are forgotten, like everybody else," he told me. This little settlement, just a wide spot in the road, sat in rolling, grassy hills - ideal Buffalo country, Boone assured me, again. He told me that buffler meat was the best-tasting wild game meat of all. They ate the same grass as cattle and elk but beef just ain't as tasty.

Belt Creek cut a deep gash - a swath through the country, exposing cliffs, ledges, and what was ordinarily the private innards of the land. Its upper area was a deep, ancient wound in the earth that had drawn miners to pan for gold, then dig shafts following narrow quartz veins of the yellow metal. But soon a thick seam of coal was discovered.

From the now-shrunken town of Belt downstream to the Missouri River, Belt Creek was stained yellow/brown to orange and had the acidity of battery acid. It looked similar to the mountain streams I had lived by in southern Arizona. Polluted by smelter and mill runoff! Purely evil, and ugly!

Belt Creek suffered high acidity, a severe decrease in the fish populations, and water quality - all of which were obvious at first glance.

When I got back to Arizona I scoured the library for information about Montana. I learned the Belt coal mine was opened in 1877, the year after Custer's defeat at the Little Big Horn, and ran for almost fifty years. Some coal was shipped overland to Fort Benton to fuel steamboats, and for use at the army post, and to heat homes. In 1893, Anaconda Mining acquired the biggest mine, Castner Coal, and coal mining peaked in the late 1890s with the construction of 100 coke ovens and a workforce of 1200 employees. The smelter in Great Falls purchased most of the coke, and the pollution of Belt Creek intensified.

Boone reminded me that along with a larger population, booze, bars, and gambling, naturally came prostitutes. (I was still mulling over the real meaning of Harlowtown.) Boone said he remembered hearing of a rancher who got married, then found out his new wife had spent some time working in a bordello, so he threw her out and got a court divorce. Not long after that, he found another soiled dove from the same bawdyhouse to take home. For some reason, he kept that one.

Just before the first world war - about twenty years after it became a state in 1899, Montana officially made prostitution illegal. Soon after police began making "busts" of bawdy houses which netted fines from some prominent people from every type of work imaginable, including miners, ranchers, policemen, lawyers, doctors, and, of course, politicians.

"Yeah, Sprout, we're all basically the same animal with different outer looks, but with the same needs and hankerin''s, and temporary female companionship is one of the strongest urges," Boone said philosophically. "Yeah, remember what we saw up at the Furrier's when that steer tried to hump the pack horse last summer? Yeah, the urge is powerful. Those fallen women were carrying on work the like of which cannot be duplicated by anybody 'except a woman. It's a specialty if ever there was one, I reckon."

"It's the same all over because people's the same - everwhere," Boone said.

"Bible people will tell you that sex corrupts the body and damns the soul, but I wonder how all them psalm singers got born? 'Course there's a risk in taking such pleasures. Ye can wind up with the worst disease - syphilis - the pox - which if you don't get cured of, will kill you. Once you know you got it, you gotta take mercury, arsenic, and sulfur."

"They say that ole Columbus and his men, after their long and lonesome first trip to the New World, took their pleasures with Indin women on the warm ocean beaches in 1492 and carried syphilis back to Europe. From there it didn't take long to explode in humans all over the world," he explained.

So maybe like tobacco, syphilis might be a sort of red man's revenge on us whites, he mused. But corn and tobacco were also wonderful gifts.

"If after being with a woman, if it burns when you pee, ya better see a doctor right quick, cuz ya probably got syphilis or the drip and either one needs medicine to cure it," he warned me.

Several smaller coal mines located on the east side of Belt Creek were still in operation. As we drove through, occasionally we would pass a dump truck full of coal heading north. Boone told me that upstream on the Belt Creek were a dozen or more small silver mines that produced a little gold as well. The mines were all clustered close around the town of Neihart. The first world war pretty much killed the small mines, due to a lack of parts for machinery, but by then, the country was all cut up, and fenced with most of the big game pretty well kilt off anyway, he said. Ruined. None of the Austins were much interested in gold and silver, anyway. They were meat and, later, scalp hunters.

The afternoon passed way too fast, mostly due to Boone's interesting palaver. In what seemed like no time we were approaching Great Falls. Boone told me he needed to stop at Hoglund's to get some work gloves, so I headed for First Avenue South. I didn't need anything, but Boone bought a couple of pairs of gloves and some socks.

As we drove through town Boone spotted a horribly fat woman walking down the sidewalk on our side of the street and remarked, "Jest look at that, Sprout. That poor gal looks like a sack of cats headed for the river, poor thing. You better hope you never marry a woman and then she turns out like that one. Always get a good look at any gal's mother, cuz that's a purty sure sign of how she will be later on."

Boone told me that the top floor of Hoglund's used to house a bordello.

Boone's description of that woman's rolls and bulbs of belly blubber trying to get out of her dress has stuck with me for more than sixty years.

We stopped at Bill's service station to pick up the welded pieces. When Bill saw my face, which by then was swollen so much my left eye was just a small slit, he asked what kind of trouble we'd managed to get ourselves into in the last twenty-four hours.

Boon related the incident, praising me for my part, but actually, I had done nothing more than serve as an unwitting punching bag.

Bill said he hoped that after the unusual skunk incident and me getting smacked, he hoped there would be no number three, as bad luck usually comes in threes. So we'd best be careful, at least until well after sundown.

I returned the extra spare tire Bill had loaned us. He told us Peck had called and left word for me to drop one of the repaired mower pieces off at the Whitmore place on our way home. The local ranch manager was sitting on the steps smoking and told me to take the piece to the shop. That lazy bum never even got off his butt.

Just as we passed old Harry Baseta's little place, the jeep rounded a corner and a large mule deer doe darted across the road. I slowed down, but barely missed her. Then another doe with a fawn crossed in front of us. Well, I hoped I had avoided Bill's number three.

We were headed for Hound Creek with me planning to milk the cow after supper. I felt more tired than I would have after a really hard day of physical work. I felt like I had walked or run all day long in a stiff wind.

We stopped by the shop and unloaded the remaining welded mower piece and drove up to the cookhouse at about seven thirty that evening. Supper was normally served at six o'clock sharp. Stan came out of Peck and Vera's house and told me he had milked the cow. Then he paused to scrutinize my face. He asked me if we had run into thunder or what had mashed my head up so much.

"It warn't Sprout's fault, Stan. We run into a couple of them Skelton's and one sucker punched the Sprout whilst he was holding the door for me and Hannah. Then the local sheriff came along and jailed them two outlaws," Boone reported.

"Well, we can hear all the details later. You boys get washed up, the cook's holding some supper warm for you," my uncle told us.

As we ate our supper, Peck and Vera came along with Stan to hear the story. Again, Boone told the tale true and Peck just shook his head. No mention of the bad guys' name was made because the cook was close to the kitchen and she was grandmother to that family. Vera inspected my swollen face and said maybe I should see a doctor in the morning. Ladies are like that.

I assured everyone that I would be fine. I didn't want to lose a working day or have to pay any big doctor bills.

Peck asked if we had driven through Utica, to which I replied that we didn't figure we had time, but I would sure like to do that someday.

Peck told us that Sapphires had been found in Yogo Gulch, near Utica, in the Little Belt Mountains, of which Hound Creek was a part. He said Yogo Sapphires are the finest in the world and more gem-quality sapphires are produced in Montana than anywhere else in North America.

Just as Diamonds are a form of plain old pure carbon, Sapphires are a form of aluminum and most have a blue cornflower color, he said.

Yogo sapphires were found along with gold panned on Yogo Creek. That area was in the country of the Blackfeet, known to be the most ruthless and savage of all Indins. (They were the ones that tortured and killed Boone's brother, Mike, and plenty of other whites.) But by the time sapphires were discovered and recognized to be valuable in the mid-1890s, due primarily to the loss of buffalo, and conflicts with the U.S. military, the Blackfeet had vacated the area for points north where they joined up with their relatives, the Bloods, and Piegans.

I could sit and listen to Peck's stories forever. He, like Boone, had seen and made a lot of history in his more than eighty years in Montana. I felt lucky to be able to listen to those old men. I wished that I had been with them and men like Lewis and Clark on their adventures. But then, I was glad I still had most of my life in front of me.

The warm meal really made me sleepy and after a healthy snort of Old Grandad with the men - this time I indulged in two, I excused myself and tucked in. With my left cheek swollen and sore, I slept on my right side. I didn't even hear Boone when he came in. I enjoyed the sleep of the tuckered and spent, if not the just.

Peck figured he had time to take Boone back to Elk Horn, so I was back behind the rake team on Wednesday. I was hoping the sunshine would help reduce the vivid technicolor of my face.

By Thursday my left cheek was deep purple and really nasty looking, but the swelling around my eye was less. I noticed that almost everybody caught themselves staring at me. I was kind of tired of living this half-tone existence.

Gradually the purple faded to blue, then, after more than a week, pale green, and finally pale yellow and brown. I was thinking that a vane woman would have been buying a lot of make-up stuff to deal with a bruise like mine.

Within two weeks the color was almost normal, but I had a hardened lump beneath my eye that persisted for more than a month.

Now, more than sixty years later, I always think of that incident and watch for who or what might be coming, when I open the door for someone.

## TO THE WHITMORE

The foreman down at the Whitmore place called Peck and reported that several men of his haying crew had quit on him, so Peck sent Stan and me down to try to get the operation back in stride. It was the first time I ever worked with a team of mules. I noticed that mules even smell a little different than horses, but they sure were plenty tough and had stamina that seemed greater than most horses showed. Those mules were friendly and trustworthy, I decided. They seemed to be more sure-footed, too. I decided that I liked mules, maybe because almost everybody spoke ill of them, in spite of their good points. That seemed like pure, unfounded prejudice to me. One should give everyone and every critter their due. The bunkhouse at that ranch was far smellier than the mules. But then, some things never change.

Stan only stayed one day, then he went back to Hound Creek, but I was destined to be stuck at the Whitmore for a week or longer.

But the manager for that part of the ranch company, Bud, had less get up and go than anyone I could remember. He would begin each day at the breakfast table with a stretch and a yawn, followed by "Oh Hell," or something foul. He wore glasses and thought of himself as being a really smart cookie, but along with being lazy, he was about as sharp as a marble. He let us all know that he was a straight-ticket Democrat. I commented that where I was from they were called Damned Old Rats. He didn't respond to my impertinence, but the crew laughed. Right then and there I knew I was stronger by nature than he was. He held absolutely no hold or influence on the hired men. I think none of them had any respect for Bud, nor did I.

One evening I came in following the "after supper chores" to find a stranger - a newly hired skid-row bum - in my bunk, wrapped up in his boozy daze in my sleeping bag. I grabbed the toe end of the bag and spilled him out on the floor. He came up spitting mad and I told him to keep out of my sleeping roll and my stuff. He was about thirty-five, a tad shorter, but stouter built than me, however, he just cussed me and shuffled off to another bunk. I've never tolerated anyone else using my sleeping bag. One of the other crewmen said I was too "perticular". I didn't care what anybody thought on that score. I had enough stink of my own and had no need of a share of anybody else's.

The atmosphere of the place was sure uncomfortable, mainly due to the laziness and disinterested attitude of the manager. He was a pure pessimist and clearly didn't like to work. His attitude affected everyone around him like a horrible plague. He made the whole operation at the Whitmore an uncomfortable struggle. A person who shows no personal discipline or standards, like Bud, can never be an effective leader or boss and should be replaced as soon as possible. I mentioned that to Stan and he just nodded.

A huge Clydesdale gelding named Big Sandy stayed at the Whitmore and was probably one of the most beautiful workhorses I ever saw. He stood nineteen hands tall (6.3 feet at the withers) and weighed around a ton. But he could get ornery. In the stall, the big beast would sidestep up close and thrust his bulk against me, pinning me to the wall and squeezing the air right out of my lungs. I was cautioned that he was a kicker, too, so I gave him plenty of distance. A horse as powerful as that could easily kill a person with even a somewhat misplaced kick. But, man, could he ever pull - and that's why Stan and Peck tolerated his orneriness. He was the strongest horse I ever saw. His usual teammate, Steamboat, was a Clydesdale too, and nearly as big and strong, but he was gentle-natured. I could ride Steamboat back from the field like a saddle horse, but I never would have tried that with Big Sandy.

We'd been getting a lot of heavy rain and one evening the Whitmore manager, Bud, and the boss from the county road maintenance crew came into the bunkhouse. The county road grader's service truck had become solidly stuck in the mud just off the road about two miles from the ranch and the crew needed help getting it back on the road. He asked if we had a tractor to pull his large truck free of the gumbo mud. Bud just stood there saying nothing, like the lazy dummy he was.

Big Sandy, a Clydesdale, stands peacefully.

As I was just hand-rubbing warm oil onto my chaps, I said I could help. I suggested that I hook up Steamboat and Sandy, as I doubted we could do much good with any wheeled vehicle as bad as the road was.

Bud had been drinking and said if I wanted to do it, to go ahead, but he doubted any two horses could pull that big rig free.

The county man didn't know beans about horses so I told him to wait at the wagon while I harnessed the horses and hitched them up. I thought about taking the team of mules, too, but the county guy would not know how to drive them. The county government man even seemed scared of horses. I figured we could get the mules or another team later if needed and, if necessary, I could figure out how to drive two teams with no one else accustomed to using horses. I threw a couple of heavy logging chains in the back of the wagon and we were off. We went up the road and when we got to the truck, three other men were there with shovels in hand but had not budged the big rig which had slipped sideways off of a curve and was in a ditch making it about four or five feet below the road base. It would have to be pulled out the way it went in. A flashlight revealed the left-hand dual wheels were buried up to the axel in the sticky mud. I noticed that the front axle had no differential, so that meant there would be no power to those wheels.

The county employees were already pretty well covered with mud, so I told them to loop the heavy chain around the rear axle and I hooked the double tree to the end of the chain. About eighteen feet separated the horses from the back of the truck. I drove the team by holding the lines from the ground behind Steamboat. I was on foot and stayed well clear of kicking distance from Big Sandy. When I told the county man to start up the truck it backfired and Sandy gave a double leg kick. That startled the normally placid Steamboat and both horses lurched forward. The two-ton yank of spooked horseflesh moved the truck, but only a little.

After calming the horses, I told one of the men to tell the truck driver to leave the engine running to avoid another backfire. Then the crewman would give a hand signal to the driver to gently give it gas as I told the horses to go. I cautioned the driver to not pump the gas pedal as that might bring on another backfire. We got that heavy piece of modern machinery out of the gumbo mud mess on the third try, after the driver managed to not spin his wheels. The crew boss said they would drive back the way they had come, where the road was better, and handed me a ten-dollar bill. I hadn't expected anything other than maybe a handshake and a thank you. That was a huge tip in 1959. I assumed the country would pay the boss back for it if he ever admitted he'd gotten himself in such a jam.

The next evening right after supper I pulled a trout fisherman's pick-up out of a mud hole closer to the ranch using that big team of Clydesdales. That job was easy to do with such powerful horses and the smaller vehicle. That guy gave me ten bucks, too. I seemed to be doing well by doing good.

## THE BELLY RUB

Lucky for me, Stan came down and picked me up to go with him to Elkhorn after about a week. It was a Saturday and Stan told me that one of these weekends we'd just have to go to town for a "belly rub". That sounded great to me. I envisioned a trip to Harlowtown, over in the Judith Basin country, and a visit to a bawdy house. I'd heard men in the bunkhouse refer to the place as Harlot Town. That little trip seemed like a great way to see some new country and have a good ride, too, Stan told me. I figured the most interesting ride would be on a hired female human mattress-back, but I kept my thoughts to myself. It would be a double-header of new experiences for me. The thought of that special weekend and visiting a real "professional" lady visited my consciousness and dominated my schoolboy daydreams for the rest of the summer. If my uncle Stan sanctioned it, it must be okay, I reasoned. I had visions of a Kitty-like woman from the Long Branch Saloon, right out of "Gunsmoke", standing at the entrance to greet and treat us eager young cowboys. But the trip never took place.

After more than a year I asked Stan about that "belly rub" he was going to take me on. He explained to me that was the local term for a dance. I'm sure Stan knew all along what I was dreaming, and he no doubt enjoyed the intentional misunderstanding. Shucks, I sure had a different expectation! My seventeen-year-old hormones had been working overtime.

## ALL TIED UP

On my once-monthly trips to Great Falls to get my Bicillin shots I always had things to pick up for the ranch. I guess that justified my receiving full payment on my shot days. On the July 1959 trip, I was to stop by the house of an acquaintance of Peck Wareheim's to pick up a couple of reportedly good hands to help with haying.

When I arrived, a third man had turned up and was asking for a job. He claimed to be a hard worker. This fellow was of medium build and appeared to be about twenty-five years old - about half the age of the other two men. He was clean and friendly enough, not too fat or too skinny, about five feet, eight inches tall, and he moved well. He did not smell of booze and had no cigarettes with him, but something about this guy just seemed not quite right to me. Maybe I sensed a touch of arrogance in the guy. Peck's old friend was almost insistent that I take the fellow, so in spite of my vague reservations, I relented and said he could come along. There was plenty of room in the back of the truck.

Anyway, I figured Peck would put him to work on a trial basis, and if he proved up, the guy would have employment, good food, and decent surroundings. I figured the worst that could happen would be the fellow would turn out to be worthless and would soon get a ride to Cascade on the next trip to town. That summer we'd had a higher-than-usual rate of turnover in the haying crew.

The main stock truck.

I was driving the old International stock truck with only supplies in the back. No animals on this trip. The young guy wound up in the cab with me, while the older fellows snoozed amongst the boxes and bags of supplies in the back.

Right off, I realized this guy talked way too much. This would not wear well with Stan or Peck, or me. To hear him tell it, he was a top-notch cowboy with vast experience and natural instincts around cattle, horses, stock dogs, and anything else to do with a ranch. Of course, he claimed to be great with gasoline engines and other mechanical issues. I'd encountered bragging like his before and never liked it. He could show his "stuff" on the job - if he actually had anything to show.

As we drove along he started in with his vast, unparalleled experiences with women. Long before I had turned a teenager, I had heard others express some of these same fantasies. As my uncle Stan would say, when he opened his mouth, his brains ran out …. and it wasn't pretty to see. At my relatively inexperienced age, his stories sounded like commonly told fabrications, or exaggerations, at least.

So I wondered why he was trying so hard to impress me - a seventeen-year-old kid. Before half of the drive back to Hound Creek was done, I was wishing I had not allowed him to come along.

When we got to the ranch, I told the new guy to report to the main house, ask for Mr. Wareheim, and explain why he was there and ask for a job on the haying crew.

At supper that evening all three new hands were served and afterward showed their places in the bunkhouse.

The young guy called himself Roy Smith, but I was beginning to doubt everything he said, even his name.

Stan put Roy to driving the stacker team, a pretty easy job, but it did require paying attention to how a load of hay landed on the stack. A fast walk with the team would send the hay to the back of the stack, while a slow walk would allow the hay to slide off near the front of the pile. The two older men on the stack could be pretty direct with their comments when the loads were not going where they should. The big horses on the stacker team, Steamboat and Sally, were experienced and responsive to whoever was driving them.

For that week I was happy to be driving the two faster teams as I raked and bunched the freshly cut hay. I always preferred silence or the creek of harness leather to bragadoccio coming from any jerk's mouth.

But Roy asked for more challenging work, like running the motorized bull rake. After a couple of days of expressing his desire, after supper one evening I heard Peck tell Stan to try him out on the rake, but if he displayed any "Barney Oldfield" high-speed maneuvers, he was to go back to the stacker team. We didn't need to be spending prime time replacing rake teeth and other broken stuff.

Then I knew what it was about Roy that disturbed me. His hair was too well-kept. Before meal times he would always wet down his locks and comb his hair just so. Anybody that spends too much time on his hair .... well, that has always made them suspicious to me.

Well, Roy didn't even last through the first afternoon. After about an hour of pushing hay reasonably well, he tried one abrupt turn at high speed and went flying off the seat, landing in the fresh-cut alfalfa stubble. The machine continued a short distance and stalled as the rake teeth dug into the dirt. His unseating happened close to the stack. It seemed he was feeling cocky and was trying to show off his driving skills to everybody. When he pulled himself together and stood up, he was bent over toward his left side and holding his ribs.

That trick earned him his place back driving the stacker team.

After supper that evening some of the older fellows had some shaming comments for Roy. They asked him where he got all his experience driving gasoline engines and if he'd ever been aboard a saddle bronc.

Roy knew he was being ridiculed and he didn't like it. He had been "found out". I think he began to spend even more time getting his hair combed just right. He had a seriously over-inflated opinion of himself.

In spite of his loss of credibility, Roy kept exercising his jaws and imagination even more than before his unseating from the bull rake. He was looking for attention, seemed to me.

Most evenings after supper Roy would go lay in his bunk, often bumming smokes off the other men.

One evening, just before dark, Stan came to my little cabin and told me he needed help in the shop, so I should gather up Roy and come over. Roy was not in his bunk, so I got another fellow.

We finished the little job in the shop and headed back to our bunks. As we passed by the barn Stan heard a noise in the tack room. When we went in, we found Roy had put a saddle near the back door, with a pile of tools - fence pliers, hoof trimmers, and hobbles in a cardboard box. It looked like he was planning to take off with the stuff.

Stan asked him what he had in mind. We caught Roy off guard and he stammered as he cobbled together a story of how he planned to take the saddle over to the bunkhouse and oil it.

"You planning to oil that other stuff, too?", asked Stan. My Uncle Stan was really angry.

Roy lost his cool and started stuttering and jabbering, making no sense. Stan said he figured we'd better use the hobbles on Roy and take him to town in the morning.

So despite Roy's protests, Abe and I restrained Roy as Stan tied his hands behind his back and lashed his feet together, then pushed him onto the floor. He would have a tough time getting up, tied as he was. Stan told him if he didn't keep his mouth shut, he would gag him, as well.

Roy spent the night tied up and on the floor. He didn't get released for breakfast, but Stan escorted him to the jeep and Peck drove him to Cascade. Roy was canned.

## EXPLORING ON A DAY OFF

We were blessed with really fine weather that summer and things were going so well, that at breakfast one Sunday, Peck announced that we could all take the day off. The men in the crew shuffled back to their bunkhouse, no doubt to loaf, smoke, read comic books, and maybe gamble a little. Complaining about ex-wives was a common waste of time for many of them. Some of their stories, such as the one told about counting his wife's pubic hairs, were a bit too raw and personal for me. I doubt any of them had any liquor secreted near their bunks from the last brief trip to Great Falls, but if they did, it would surely surface that afternoon.

I asked Vera if she wanted some grasshoppers, but she had plans to visit a neighbor, so I saddled up Reuben and headed down the Little Hound Creek toward the Main Hound, which fed into the Smith River and eventually to the Missouri River a few miles upstream from the big town of Great Falls. It was my first time in that country. I had the pump .22 rifle for groundhogs, but never fired a shot that day. I did jump a whitetail buck whose antlers were impressive but still covered in velvet. These northern whitetails were huge compared with the diminutive Coes whitetails I had been around in Arizona and New Mexico. I wanted to hunt them, but I would have to be back in Arizona before the season opened here. Most of the deer thereabouts were Mulies, so seeing a Whitetail was noteworthy. When we took Stan's ashes to scatter at Hound Creek in 2008 we saw primarily Whitetails, which are reported to be displacing Mule deer all over the west.

Peck, Stan, and Boone all had casually mentioned occasionally finding a buffalo carcass here and there. What they referred to as a carcass was mostly just some scattered bones, but I had never seen a sign of anything like that. The bones had to have been fifty to seventy years old or even older. My eyes were always peeled for almost anything like that. I would usually vary my routes in case I could find or see something new. Every chance I got, I would ride or walk up to any prominent hill and look for flint chips, indicating some Indian had knapped out some arrowheads as he sat there, so long ago. I did locate a couple of sites that afternoon, but I found only flakes. No intact projectile points came to my view. Geographically, good observation spots don't change much over time. Good places to sit and look for wild game don't change from one generation to the next.

Fishing was pretty good with the native Rainbows being completely unaccustomed to fishermen down the creek I caught about fifteen, releasing all but one of fourteen inches that I cooked on a stick and ate as Reuben nibbled on the good virgin grass. I always liked to try to live off the land as much as possible. This was a good life and I figured I would remain a cowboy, but I sure wanted to figure out how to someway get a place of our own for Stan and me. Stan and I worked hard and enjoyed almost all of the work - even shoveling horse poop, but it would be so much better to be working for primarily our own family benefit.

As always when in a new area, I was trying to take it all in, knowing, even fearing, that I might never get back that way again. As I was headed home to the ranch, I took a short ride up a little side canyon, near where I'd jumped the whitetail buck. I was primarily looking for shed deer antlers. Then, near the creek at the base of a tree, I saw a buffalo skull. I couldn't believe my eyes! It was a huge bull skull, in great condition, apparently washed out of a stream bank that spring and dropped when the water level was higher. No porcupine or small rodent had chewed either horn or any bone. Wow! What luck!

What a find! I was speechless and happy beyond description.

It crossed my mind that the Indians whose flint chips I picked up might have seen or hunted this very same critter. Maybe they even killed and ate it. I wondered how bison meat tasted, and I knew that it was bound to be good. Boone proclaimed it better than the best beefsteak. How I wished I could have taken part in a wild buffalo hunt, maybe a wild Indian fight, too. Daydreams have always entered my thoughts, especially when alone out in the country. It's a form of self-entertainment, I guess.

Needless to say, I took the skull back to the ranch, tied on behind my saddle. No one but me thought it was that big a deal. It was just useless old junk to them. They'd seen it all before. But, I kept it in the little cabin with me and admired it often. I took it with me when I went back to the desert in September.

## BACK TO ELKHORN

We spent a couple of days doing routine things, mostly servicing equipment at the Little Hound Creek place before Stan and I headed up to Elkhorn in the jeep. We loaded the back end up with salt blocks and other supplies such as groceries for us and Boone. We put in a box of framing and siding nails to tack a new cabin together when time permitted. A truckload of lumber, siding, and other materials had been delivered earlier that month. Our main objective was to gather up cull heifers that had been bob-tailed and move them down to the rail head in Cascade. That would mean a forty-mile trip to the Little Hound Creek, then another twenty or so miles to the Whitmore, and finally the leg to Cascade - another twenty miles or so. This also meant a solid week or more of the type of work that I longed for. I could hardly wait!

As we drove out the gate the sunshine and the smells of Montana - horses, cattle and their droppings, and grass - fueled my enthusiasm. We were in for some wonderful times - I just knew it. I got the last gate closed and climbed in as Stan drove up the road. Just short of the cabin, we rounded a sharp bend and found ourselves next to a dandy big black bear that seemed to be no more than mildly curious at our sudden appearance. Murphy was no doubt laughing his head off, as we did not have a rifle in the jeep! This would have been a perfect opportunity to get the bear - it was probably the big boar that Boone said kept hanging around the old cabin for the last two years, but we weren't prepared. Ratz! But, I did have my Brownie box camera with me and it was on the seat next to me that time.

What woulda, coulda, and shoulda been my first black bear kill.

Nice as he looked, being August, the hide would not have gone through the tanning well, if at all. The inside of the hides of the few marmots I skinned in July and August were dark - not the milky white color of a good quality winter skin, so I'd quit skinning them. Tanning would probably have caused the bear's hair to fall out in patches. But I would have been happy to kill that bear, anyway. And I would have had the skull and the memories, and I would have eaten some of its meat.

The bear swung his head right and left as he appraised us, then turned and sauntered slowly into the woods. Stan drove on, with both of us just shaking our heads.

## HUNTING CULLS

Selecting the cull animals was a much tougher job on the open range than if they were not so wild and free, but we cut out thirty-seven head of reject heifers and held them in a small fenced pasture along the road that led back down to Hound Creek. With such a small bunch, Stan figured we may as well add more critters, so we scouted up as many three-year-old steers as we could locate and found some that were even older. A couple of them was maybe even five years old that had eluded previous round-ups and overwintered on their own. These were much bigger animals, but they would bring a reduced price per pound. Peck was happy to get twenty-three cents a pound (live weight) for the two-year-old steers. That would make a steer worth less than two hundred dollars. I never did hear what the older stuff brought. I could appreciate the lower price for older, tougher animals, but I never could understand why a registered Hereford would bring more money than a steer of mixed breed. I was puzzled by that issue quite a lot. All the beef stock was put into feed lots before slaughter and once butchered, the meat all looked the same to me. Tough meat never bothered me either, for that matter. Most of the venison we ate at home was more chewy than store-bought meat of any kind.

Elkhorn looked a lot different in August than it had in late May.

After five days, we had about a hundred head of cattle, including cull cows with their calves, and a bull with a broken penis, ready to trail down to Little Hound Creek. The most common penile injury in breeding bulls is penile hematoma (broken penis). Rather than just a small vessel rupture, these are generally large ruptures. It puts the proud bull out of business - painfully.

The old Elkhorn place and fences were in decent shape and Boone was ready for some solitude. I figured he smoked, drank before the bottle went dry, and mostly daydreamed of fighting Indians when he was by himself, which anymore was most of the time, both summer and winter.

The trailing went easy with one overnight stop. Some of the cows were lamed up a bit, which is why they would be sold. The limpers set the pace slower than normal, but I didn't mind that.

I came upon two large rattlesnakes and killed them both. I suggested taking them with us to skin later and taste after boiling them up with garlic and dipping them in melted butter, but Stan wasn't interested in eating any snake. After all, we had beef!

## A ROCK IN THE FROG

One hot, humid afternoon as I was using the dump rake to windrow and bunch freshly cut hay, the gelding, Pete, seemed to stumble, then he walked with what appeared to be a painful limp. The first thought that flashed through my mind was ... rattlesnake. Pete was really spooky around snakes. The mare in the team, Millie, seemed to be aware of Pete's difficulty, and him not pulling his share of the load. She kicked at him, but the tongue of the rake blocked her thrust.

After a hundred yards or so of his limping, with no sign of a snake, I stopped the team. I told them "Whoa" and unhooked the tug lines (traces) before I walked alongside Pete, talking softly and running my hand along his side.

It seemed like he had a problem with his right hind foot. As he was on the right side of the team, that foot was on the outside, not next to the tongue, which made it easy to access. But Pete was always a bit twitchy, so I talked soothingly to him and patted his cheek before I leaned down to lift his front foot by the long hairs of the fetlock. There was nothing abnormal to see with that foot. I wanted to relax Pete. I continued to talk gently to the gelding as I moved back to lift his hind foot. Pete did not like me messing with his hind foot, but after several attempts with him dodging, and dancing, I got it up and found the problem. Somehow a smooth rock had become wedged in between the frog and the side of the horseshoe. I noticed this was a smooth rock - a stream polished slick. How that had been picked up in the mountain hayfield was a mystery to me. It must have happened in the creek that morning.

With Pete's foot resting on my bent knee, I fished the pocket knife out of my pants and used it to dislodge the offending rock. I broke a half inch off the tip of my blade on the first try, then used the remaining part to pry loose the rock. That foot was obviously tender and Pete flinched each time I put pressure on the rock. When the rock popped free, I suspect Pete and I were equally relieved. There was no blood. I put the rock in my pocket to show Stan.

I hooked up the tugs and continued with raking the last of the cut hay, but Pete kept favoring that sore foot. He kept dancing around, which irritated Millie. We had another two hours of work to finish the field, but it was only a half hour before quitting time, so I elected to go back to the stacker and minimize the chance of getting Pete seriously lamed up.

Old Sully was driving the stacker team and I told him what had happened as I took a pull on the water jug. He said he thought it was a good idea to not push Pete too much. Pete was an honest horse, though a bit skittish.

I left the rake in the field and led Pete and Millie back to the headquarters behind the wagon, which was the usual procedure.

After supper, Stan took a look at Pete's hoof and said we'd give him a day or so off, but he expected Pete and the foot would be fine. Normally in hot weather, I used Boots and Freddie in the morning, then Pete and Millie in the afternoon, but either team could work the whole day.

So Pete and Millie got a couple of days off. I wondered if they were more confused than relieved. Soon Pete was no longer favoring that foot, so it was back into the harness for him and Millie.

Stan broke and shoed all the ranch horses and taught them manners as he worked. He did not tolerate a horse leaning on him in his bentover posture as he trimmed the hoof and then nailed on the shoe. If a horse tried to lean, Stan would respond with a low base, growling "get off me" and a smack in the ribs with whatever was in his hand. The horses learned quickly. Stan was about five feet four inches tall and weighed around one hundred and fifty pounds. He was plenty tough, but no one would last long with a half-ton quarter horse, let alone a full-ton draft horse leaning on them in any posture.

Stan had never been formally trained by a licensed farrier (horse-shoer) until he moved to Arizona and went to a farrier school. He got his instruction from older ranch hands like Tom Means, who had passed away a few years before I came on the scene. Most cowboys just learned 'shoein' as a matter of necessity, whether they had the correct tools or not.

But Stan was really interested in everything he did. His usual measure for the quality of work was, "Is it as good as can be?" He had a complete set of high-quality tools, nail pullers, hoof testers, trimmers, nippers, knives, picks, rasps, hammers, clinch blocks, an anvil, a forge, pritchels (punches), tongs, nails and nail cutters, clinchers, clinch cutters, hoof gages, and other tools. He didn't use a hoof stand, he just balanced the horse's leg above his knee. He kept all his tools sharp and lubricated and he didn't care for other people using his gear.

I wanted to learn everything about ranching, so Stan put me to removing old shoes and trimming the hoof for a new shoe, but he took it from there.

Common Horseshoe

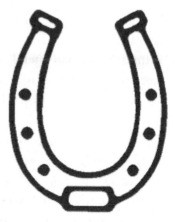

Roughshod Horseshoe

Most horseshoes are made of cast iron or steel, but aluminum is often used for race horses, and softer materials like plastic are used where indicated.

Horseshoe nails are not round. They are flattened and come with a slight bend near the tip. The bend directs the nail toward the outside of the hoof as it is hammered in place, rather than inward toward the sensitive inner tissues and the frog. Normally three or four nails are placed on each side of a horseshoe. With normal ranch use, the horseshoes needed to be replaced about every four to six weeks.

Roughshod horses sometimes had nail heads projecting from the bottom of the shoe.

Winter shoes had metal projections from the top and ends of the shoes and were held in place with eight or more nails. Some winter shoes were made with small projections or cleats around the entire perimeter of the shoe.

Stan told me he thought black hooves were tougher than white ones, but that was only one part of what makes a good horse. The average hoof grows 1/4 to 3/8 inches per month and the average hoof is 3 to 4 inches in length, so a horse grows a new hoof just about every year. Rapidly growing hooves are considered to be desirable and are easier to keep properly trimmed and shod.

A roughshod shoe I found at the little Bear Creek mine in Alaska

Stan had a book on the history of horseshoeing which I borrowed. Back when they were in common use as draft animals, oxen were often fitted for iron shoes - two shoes per foot in the case of bovines, one for each side of the cloven hoof. Stan had a couple of used ox shoes he'd found someplace years ago. They were tacked to his toolbox. I read that people had been protecting their workhorses with shoes since before the iron age. Romans used plants and rawhide hoof applications and called them "hipposandles." The Huns wove plants to protect their horse's hooves.

## THRASHING THE OATS

Several of the local ranches jointly owned and maintained an old thrashing machine and the cooperative system usually worked pretty well. Peck sent me and two others down to the next-door ranch that was harvesting their oats to help, then the thrashing machine was taken to our place along with some of the crew from the previous ranch and some from the ranch that was next in line - the crews sort of leapfrogged to expedite harvesting the oats at the optimum time. So people from the adjacent three ranches did the thrashing. We were jammed up at night. Some of the neighboring hands were interesting to share stories with. The younger ones talked about their dreams of women and girls mostly. Many of the men told almost exactly the same story. I doubted they had experienced the activities they claimed to be their own. They probably heard the stories from others. So it is with men, boys, and sex stories.

The oats were cut and bound with string before sliding off onto the ground. Then we men and boys would walk along, stack the bundles upright with cut stalks on the ground, and grain heads up, forming shocks - kind of like the stacks of rifles seen in old Civil War photos. We pulled the binder with the "Big M" tractor and then - usually the next day - walked along and set the bundles up into shocks. We all killed rattlesnakes anytime we found them ..... and lots of snakes showed up in August. I noticed that the rattlers had a musty odor like the ones I had smelled in Arizona, so figured August was likely the rutting time for these northern vipers, too. However, I read that rattlers breed in the springtime.

Stan is adjusting the string binder which was modified for use with a tractor. Notice the shocks behind and the haystack in the distance.

An oat field freshly cut and partly shocked.

It was sweaty work and always a bit twitchy, watching for snakes that came to the bundles to scarf up the mice and other small rodents drawn to the grain. It was also interesting to think about how someone with mechanical ability and vision had designed such a useful machine. It would have taken so much longer to cut and bind those bundles by hand!

To me, it was all enjoyable work, but I was relieved that we were not working on a pure oat-growing ranch. When the oats were ready, the thrashing machine was drug into place with the "Big M" tractor. We would walk along with pitchforks and toss the shocks up onto a horse-drawn wagon, which was to be pitch forked into the thrasher. A huge mountain of straw soon grew up on one side of the thrasher and later a bailer was brought in to seize the straw up into seventy-pound bales. We used pitchforks to feed the bailer, so before it was done, that straw had been handled by men five or six times. So the straw had been cut by the binder, hand stacked into shocks, allowed to dry, then pitchforked onto a trailer, then pitchforked into the thrasher, then the straw was pitchforked again into the bailer, then the bales were hand loaded onto a trailer and, finally, handled again when it was stacked and finally, the straw was scattered in stalls or wherever it was needed for bedding.

It was a very labor-intensive operation. But labor and time were cheap back in the 1950s as they had been for decades earlier.

An old-time thrashing machine, ready to be put to work.

One of the things that crossed my mind when working with oats is what the origin of "sowing his wild oats" might be. I knew it referred mostly to young men spreading their "seed" around with various females, but still, I was curious. And I never did get a satisfactory explanation. However, thoughts of trying to become a planter did frequently enter my day and night dreams. But my potential garden remained unseeded, despite my most vivid dreams.

Time was flying by way too fast and I kept dreading my inevitable return to the blighted, cactus-infested Arizona desert and that boring high school.

The new cabin at Elkhorn.

During my last week in Montana, Stan took me and a couple of the crew up to Elkhorn in the big International stock truck full of building materials, along with a wood cooking stove and other materials for the new cabin. We had a graph paper plan - a homemade blueprint of sorts, drawn out by Stan and Peck. One of the crewmen knew carpentry pretty well. Stan was handy with building stuff. Most people in those days did their own building, especially if it was simple frame construction. In three days we had the cabin enclosed with a roof in place. It sure was an improvement over the ancient log homesteader's place which no doubt had taken a lot more time to build with raw logs a hundred or so years before. I kept dreaming of the elk hunts that would be taking place right from that cabin a couple of months after I had to depart for the scorched southern desert.

By late August, I was worked down pretty thin and looked like a convict. I'm next to "my" cabin, behind Stan's with the spring house and Peck and Vera's house in the far background.

## SEPTEMBER 1959

Having good school grades and performance I had been able to talk Dad, Mom, and Stan into letting me return to school a full two weeks late. I had to promise them that I would make serious efforts to catch up quickly and maintain my good grades, and I would do my level best to try to avoid fistfighting. Based on my recent history, both in Montana and at home, they agreed to my extra time at the ranch. And at five dollars a day, I could also put an extra seventy dollars in my savings account. But the day came way too soon for me to pack up and head south for my senior year in high school. As before, I had an inner fear that somehow, some evil might prevent me from ever returning to that wonderful ranch life in Montana.

## SENIOR YEAR IN HIGH SCHOOL

My senior year at San Manuel High School was, somehow, a lot of fun. I had plenty of self-confidence and retained my natural reaction to bullies and abuse of power by authorities, which inevitably led me into some relatively minor pugilistic confrontations and one suspension for "mouthing off" to a teacher. He deserved it, of course. He was an idiot, too. How the devil such stupid and evil people get into positions of power and influence is something I've never figured out. Many years later I read the book "The Peter Principle" which attempts to explain how people tend to be promoted beyond their abilities, especially in bureaucracies. One of the main reasons jerks get ahead in government is that after they've proved themselves to be bad, they just keep getting promotions to rid their co-workers of their foolery. I figure once someone shows they're really bad, dishonest, or incompetent, that should be it for the jerk. They should be shunned and done with.

I'd heard the old adage that "cream rises to the top", but I decided that with people, that may be true, but I had noticed that equally true is "some turds rise faster and float higher."

A teacher, I'll refer to him as Mr. Baloney served as librarian and baseball coach. He always seemed to be intellectually impaired, which coupled with his large physical stature helped propel him into the dumb bully category. The other kids had him figured out to be a dumbo, too.

I always figured it was okay to be dumb - nobody chooses that - but it's never okay to be ornery. A person can't just decide to be smart, but he can and surely should control his ornery side. Part of the problem is that too many dumb people don't recognize just how pathetically dumb they really are.

I read a lot of books and never was late in turning any of them in. Library fines or other such drains on my limited economy were unconscionably wasteful. I was saving up - maybe for a ranch in Montana someday.

I had read all of Teddy Roosevelt's books on his time as a cowboy on his ranch in North Dakota, as well as his hunting travels to Africa and South America and I went to the school library to look for a book on his politics. As I was checking out a new book, the oppressive librarian/coach blustered up to me and told me that I had been late with a book. I looked at him and told him that was not so, as I made certain to either renew my loan or turn in all my books on time. When I approached the desk to check out another book, the jerk handed me a slip indicating that I owed two dollars and fifteen cents and had to pay that before I could borrow another book.

I told the guy that I wasn't going to pay any fine, as I owed nothing at all.

That put the jerk into a rage and he hollered that I wasn't going to get away with that. He seemed to never waste an opportunity to show how stupid he really was.

As I could feel my face getting red and was ready to let the guy have it, verbally, one of the girls working in the library came forth.

"Mr.Baloney, Jake did turn the book in on time, it's right here and the turn-in date is recorded on the slip", she said.

"Well, Mr.Jacobson, you're lucky," said Balone.

"No, I'm not just lucky, I am right and you're a wanna-be bullying idiot," was my spontaneous reply.

Balone reached as if to grab me by the shoulder and I dodged his hand. Our confrontation had drawn everyone's attention. The peace and quiet of the library were thoroughly compromised.

"Get out of here, Jacobson, and go to the office, you're expelled!", was the explosive response from Baloney. I was confirmed in my suspicion that old Balone never did like me very much.

"You're still a blooming idiot, Mr. Baloney, Just take a look at yourself in the mirror, sometime," I said as I backed out, never taking my eyes off him. I was ready to fight the big, ornery fool.

So, I got furloughed for the rest of the week, which only had two days left in it, anyway. I figured I got awarded a four-day weekend. I was charged with insubordination. I never felt like the rest of the school administration and teaching staff sided with Baloney in their hearts, but they kept out of the conflict. Birds of a feather stick together, you know, wherever you find them. Plus I could have said less, but I took great personal satisfaction in what I had told the jerk. I took Pop's 1955 Chevy pick-up back into the Galliuro Mountains and had a wonderful time camping out with our dog Gyp, and glassing deer as I ruminated over the injustices of life amongst most other people and the inevitable injustices of society in general. I debated with mysel on how to avoid conflicts that are so common between people and decided the best bet was to limit how much I had to be involved with people I didn't care for. Most of all, as much as possible I needed to not depend on others. Maybe, in my case, that applied to most people in general.

Any day of huntin' beats the best day in school.

It was Javalina season, so I hunted for one of them, too, using my Dad's German eight-millimeter Mauser. I saw a lot of pigs and shot a dandy old boar with impressive, long canine teeth.

But, overall, I didn't have too many conflicts during my senior year and was made "Annual King" of San Manuel High School - to the surprise of many - most of all, myself. At the graduation ceremonies, the Principal mentioned how the graduates would be heading out into the world and one he was sure would go up north to be a "bull in Montana". That got some chuckles from the crowd.

## SUMMER, 1960

Since it was graduation time, those in power wouldn't let me skip out early that year, I had to stay to endure the ceremonies and all, but I was wishing I was back on the ranch. I never did enjoy ceremonies or rituals of any kind, including those in church and the Boy Scouts.

So, the day after high school graduation I bid our fine dog, Gyp, goodbye, and I was once again on a DC-3, headed back to Little Hound Creek. The smells that greeted me when I deplaned were by now, part of my being. I knew I was home! My ambition to own a ranch in that part of Montana grew more intense. Just how to do that was always on my mind. I concluded that I would likely have to leave the ranch to earn enough money to ever buy one. I had a dream once about robbing a bank, but woke up and realized that nightmare route would never tempt me. Gambling seemed like too much of a long shot and I'd never heard of a big lottery. Somehow I would have to earn the money, but at five bucks a day, the chances of that leading to ownership of even a small ranch were slim to non-existent. Maybe I could scout up a fine woman with a dandy ranch and come by it that way. But that seemed unlikely and much too sleazy.

I had quizzed Stan about having our own place. He said we'd about have to run a hundred head of mother cows to make a decent living with a cow/calf outfit, and that would be possible only if our bank loan payments were not too high.

Added to that, that pretty girl from down the road, hadn't liked my choice of jewelry, so that was a no-go for me.

Stan met me and we did the usual ranch supply shopping. Again he asked me about my feet, but I was not going to buy any more cowboy boots. This time I found a pair of Blucher Boot knock-offs for sixteen dollars. They were lace boots with good heels suitable for wearing spurs - much more practical than those pointy-toed cowboy boots, which by then were pretty well worn out and never had been that comfortable. If I'd been wearing Blucher boots I could have stomped that ornery Eddie just as effectively.

We got cheeseburgers for lunch and beat it on back to the ranch by mid-afternoon, as the ranch was operating with a full crew of hired hands and there was always more than plenty to do that time of year.

Due to my graduation, I was almost three weeks later this year than I'd been the year before, so I had missed the long spring cattle drives, branding, and other favored chores, but I was in time for all of the fence-mending and pole cutting at Elkhorn. Boone was still there, of course, and at ninety years of age he hadn't run out of stories yet. All his stories fascinated me, even those that he told multiple times. His repeated stories were the same as the original tellings, so I was as sure as I could be that they must be at least mostly true. Stan left me with Boone for about a week at Elkhorn, riding fence lines and stacking lodge pole pine for bull rake and farm hand teeth, with a few larger ones for replacing wagon tongues. It seemed like a graduation present to me. It was a great introduction to what I expected to be doing for the rest of my life - right there on that same ranch - THE ranch, in my world. I kept puzzling about how we might ever be able to afford a ranch of our own. I mused that it was probably a shame that girl whose Dad loaned us the boar hog didn't fall in love with the rattlesnake necklace I had offered her. I dreamed once that I found a stash of gold bullion hidden by stagecoach robbers, but woke up way too soon from that one.

## BULL RIDIN'

Neither my uncle Stan nor Peck Wareheim had any interest in, or use for rodeo cowboys. According to them, rodeo performers were just show-offs and did not make for dependable ranch hands. In fact, if a potential ranch hand mentioned that he had done some rodeoing, he would be put to close scrutiny and in many cases, he would not be hired to work for the Staunton Ranch Company in any capacity. That was prejudice at work, but sometimes prejudice, especially if it is based on life experiences, serves one well. Most prejudices come to be, due to their accuracy. So, prejudice is a natural thing, seems to me.

As an eighteen-year-old still-wannabe cowboy, I had an interest in some of rodeo's competitive activities, especially bull and bronc riding. It might be a way to gain enough money for a down payment on a ranch of our own. Now and then I'd been given a little taste of bronc riding by surprise when I happened to be riding one of the saltier horses in the bunch, and the beast decided to unload his burden ... which was me. Each horse has its own unique personality and we had the potentially dangerous ones figured out ... like Silk or Big Sandy, the massive Clydesdale workhorse. His strength was too valuable to not use him, but we had to keep alert to avoid being squeezed in a stall, or kicked most any time, by that ornery-natured cayuse.

Stan did all the horse breaking and shoeing, for both the work-horses and those destined primarily for the saddle, and he had them all pretty well educated on what he considered to be good manners and appropriate behavior. He felt misbehavior in a horse was nothing less than dishonest, and he hated dishonesty where ever he encountered it - in man or beast.

In July of 1960, I was again spending a couple of weeks down at the Whitmore. My primary activities were mowing and raking loose hay for the over-shot stackers, alternating days with a couple of two-horse or two-mule teams. It was hot enough and work enough to substitute the team I used at noon, then work another team until dark. For some of the smaller hay plots, I would cut, then later rake the hay to the edge, so a motorized bull rake could come to pick it up or we would put it on a wagon with the farm hand, then haul it to the stack. It was extra time-consuming, but the good hay was worth the extra effort, I realized. I'd been sent down to that ranch because they were behind on haying and nobody there knew how or wanted to drive a team of horses to cut and rake the little hay plots. The gnarly areas around the braided creeks and steep side hills had been left for me to do with the horses. I had a pretty fast team of a gelding and a mare and another team of mules - a jack and a jenny, which - in character for mules - proved to be tougher and had more stamina than the horse team. The weather was hot and dry, so I would leave the barn with one team pulling the wagon and the second team tied behind, then we'd head for the section that had hay to be cut. While one team was working, the other was tethered out to feed on succulent new grass. Each team worked for half the day. I normally held the tougher mules back for the afternoon.

One evening after supper I rubbed down my teams and was putting in some copper rivets to repair the harness when up drove a semi-truck and trailer with a load of young Hereford bulls. There were sixteen of them. The driver of the truck tooted his horn several times, which drew the manager out to see what was happening. Normally right after supper the lazy manager of this part of the ranch would roll up a cigarette, start drinking and be out of sight until just before breakfast the next morning. This "after-hours" disturbance irritated the guy. I had expected him to have been replaced by someone more reliable long ago, but he still held the post of resident manager of the Whitmore.

Several of us "hands" helped place the truck ramps and unload the bulls. We were told that the bulls would remain corralled for a few days before trailing them up to Hound Creek and soon thereafter to the summer pastures at Elkhorn where they would soon get busy with their important, life-giving service work on the heifers.

The manager made a hasty return to his couch, ashtray, and booze.

There were two other teenagers working at the Whitmore at the time. They had been hired in Cascade for a couple of weeks of haying. They planned to collect their wages and be going back to town on the coming weekend. Those young fellows were pretty decent and we three "sprouts" got along well. I was the senior and more experienced one and neither of them seemed to chafe at that. Up to that point, we'd had no opportunity for mischief, as the work kept us busy and tired. But those bulls drew us all like sweet candy ... or maybe, pretty girls. We figured we just had to try riding them ... the bulls, I mean.

Knowing that Stan would never approve of using those bulls for anything but their primary purpose, I knew that if we were going to practice up to be rodeo bull riders, it had better be done soon.

We, youngsters, hung around watching the new stock, while everyone else went back to the smelly bunk house. Then one of the older hands suggested we get a withers rope and put a bull into the squeeze chute. We young fellows could take turns trying to stay aboard after the bull was released back into the corral. It sounded like a fine idea at the time. I located a small bell, not a big clanging cowbell like the real rodeos use, all we could find was one used to help locate a horse in the morning after the animal had been turned loose for the night. I tied the bell to a length of heavy manilla rope and placed it around the bull, so the bell would be hanging under the animal's belly. The young bull did not appreciate this attention, but we had him squeezed tight enough to get the job done without much risk to ourselves.

These young Herefords were not as wild as most range cattle, but all had horns, and few of the horns had been blunted. They looked somewhat formidable, but not especially dangerous or aggressive. Like most Herefords, they had bland, rather than angry-looking faces.

The first little bull's horn tips had been sawed off a little. and he didn't cotton to the idea of being jammed into the squeeze chute, but after a quarter of an hour of prodding and poking, we had him ready for the withers rope. He became really upset by the tinkling bell.

So the question arose regarding who was going to be the first to ride the raging bull. We decided to do a rock, paper, scissors procedure and I got second place, which I reckoned was lucky for me. It would give me a chance to see what might be in store for me when my time came to experience the forthcoming explosion.

One of the other kids was on the chubby side, but tough enough, we figured. His name was Bill Sheldon, but we referred to him as Billy Tubs, due to his noticeable pot belly. As he eased down on the bull, the four-legged critter began to snort, blowing snot all over as he shook his head. I wondered if the bull realized this was not part of his formal and otherwise enjoyable job description. He sure acted like

145

he knew it. The bell was jingling plenty, which jangled everybody's nerves. That bull suddenly looked a lot more dangerous than he had a few minutes before.

Me and the other kid, opened the chute door and the white-faced double-horned terror lurched free of the confines and ran straight for the rest of the bulls, slinging a flow of his fresh diarrhetic poop behind. The gang of soon-to-be breeders seemed to crowd close together as they kept focused on the one catapulting toward their midst. As the bull with the human tumor on his back reached the bunch of his peers, they parted to make room for him as he shook his head to the right and jammed a horn into Billy Tub's big gut.

Billy let out a screech but hung on until the bull made it through the bunch and abruptly stopped just short at the far side of the corral, which caused Billy to fly off over the bull's head and hit the poles of the fence. It looked like a bad wreck from where the other kid, Larry, and I were standing.

One of the few young bulls with blunted horn tips. It probably meant he had displayed an aggressive nature.

The gaggle of bulls bomb-shelled in all directions, but one abruptly turned and ran right over Billy, stepping on his thigh with one hoof as he charged by, headed for safety. It was purely an accidental trampling, but it no doubt hurt just the same as if it had been deliberately done. Billy Tubs really started hollering after that stomping.

Larry and I ran toward to rescue our fallen comrade, whooping loudly to scatter the bulls in front of us and hoping to not get gored in the process. The gang of bulls just scattered away from us. Luckily, most Hereford cattle are gentle by nature, but I kept a wary eye on the one with a ring in its nose and a glare in its eye.

This bull looked like he was not one to fool with. The ring on his nose convinced me that he had been a troublemaker.

We helped Billy to his feet as he massaged his thigh and his belly, inadvertently rubbing fresh bull diarrhea into his clothes as he did it. The urge to practice rodeo bull riding had rapidly diminished on our list of favorite things to do that evening.

Now all the young toros were keeping a close eye on us, and we were watching them.

It would have been unconscionable for me to not take my turn, however, it was something I flirted with for a moment. But no, that would be a just plain chicken thing to do. I had to take at least one ride and try to stay on longer, and unload, or be unloaded, less ignominiously than Billy had done.

This time, with Billy Tubs temporarily incapacitated, just Larry and I had the job of getting a bull into the chute. We weren't sure which one we got squeezed into the confines of the chute, but we were sure it wasn't the same critter that Billy had ridden, as it had a different pattern of fresh diarrhea smeared on its back end. After searching the barn, I located a battery-charged "hot shot" which helped us get bull number two in place. Once the buzzing sound becomes familiar to the cattle, a mere waving of the wand with an occasional short buzz puts them at full attention and on their best behavior. Cattle are smart when it comes to an electric prod pole. As bad luck would have it, my bull was the one with a ring in its nose.

I found the withers rope, with bell still tied on, lying near where Billy had been unloaded. It was trampled into the mud, cattle pee, and poop of the corral. We had to bend the bell to get it to ring, as it, like Billy, had been accidentally stepped on.

The stinky bunkhouse had no radio or television, so a couple of the more geezerly hired hands had ambled from the bunkhouse out to the corral to catch the entertainment we were about to provide.

Billy was still rubbing his sore spots but he had come back to life pretty well and wasn't going to miss seeing whatever disaster might be headed my way. He was grinning and fidgety with excitement, and no doubt anticipating that I was about to get a worse thumpin' than he had suffered. My bull looked really mean.

As I got ready to get aboard the nervous little ring-nosed bull one of the geezers hollered for me to wait, as I'd forgotten something important.

"And what's that," I asked.

"Spurs, you ain't gotcha spurs on, and no real cowboy rides bulls or broncs without spurs," he told me when I looked at him.

Before I could make an excuse, Billy had hobbled over to the barn's tack room and came back with my spurs. Nice guy. But that sealed it. Now I had to use them or lose face with everybody.

I was sure that using those spurs would be like throwing gasoline onto a fire, but I was cornered and saw no honorable way out. So I strapped 'em on, good and tight.

When I felt the semi-panicky animal under me, I resolved to just clutch as hard as I could with my legs and forget about any raking with the spurs, as I gripped the withers rope in my left hand. I wanted to survive and be able to walk and work the next day ... and.... hopefully for the rest of my life.

So the gate flew open and my bovine steed launched himself out. Like the first one, my horned mount meteored right for the collection of bulls across the corral. As I expected, the gang scattered and my bull turned right toward the fence, but just short of the poles, he turned hard to the left and actually tried to buck a couple of times, but he mostly just ran, shook his head, and slung ropes of snot right and left. We made one loop around the corral and I lifted my right leg and hopped off on the left side, as an exit to the right would have put me into the fence poles, and probably got me some bruised ribs ... or worse. I kept my feet, walked over, picked up my hat, and slapped it on my leg to get the grime off, smiling the whole time. I was stunned at my own unexpected performance, and I knew that I was one lucky fellow! I did not plan to do any repeats of my surprise performance.

Geezer number two said, "By Jingo, you stayed on for about eight seconds, Jaker! Maybe you found your callin' and could get into big money rodeoing, eh?"

"Nothin' to it," I responded to his praise.

"But I think I'll stick to regular cowboying and haying," was my reply. What good would rodeo winnings do me if I got busted up and couldn't do normal ranch chores I thought to myself.

So next it was Larry's turn. Larry was a couple of years older, quiet, and overall, a pretty decent kid, and I was hoping he wouldn't get hurt too badly. Billy Tubs was seemingly fully recovered. He was buoyed by the excitement and anticipation of seeing another guy get thrown, mortified, or mangled, no doubt.

By the time Larry got loaded on his bull, we'd forgotten to have him use spurs, but by then it was close to dark, so that was a good reason for me to not mention our omission. Besides, I was the only one who owned spurs, and like everything I owned, I wanted them to last. His bull spurted out of the chute about like the other two had done, but it made a couple of little jumps, and on the second one, Larry went head over heels off the back end. He actually did a complete flip, but went a little bit too far and landed on his butt. The bull kicked just in time to catch Larry in mid-tumble with a deflecting blow to his shoulder. When he picked himself up out of the mud and poop, Larry said the kick didn't even hurt. So he was lucky, too.

Those young bulls seemed to be as individual and independent as us young men, and they were acting at least as unpredictably as we were. I was certain that was probably due to their luck of not being castrated as a young calf. Steers seemed more predictable and a whole lot more docile. Steer voices seem to be a couple of octaves higher, too.

We figured we'd all done something, maybe even something to be proud of .. well, we could tell it proudly, anyway, and we figured we would leave it at that. In the bunkhouse Geezer number two offered first me, then the other kids, a pull on his jug of "Old Bust Head" as he called his hooch. I noticed that it didn't have a federal liquor tax stamp on it. I took a cautious little snort of the awful stuff and tried not to make a grimace or a wince. Its smell and taste reminded me of something I'd whiffed in the high school chemistry lab. Old Boone's bottle didn't have a tax stamp on it either, but it didn't taste as raw and chemical-laced as this vile liquid. I imagined it might be as powerful a disinfectant as Clorox or Pine-sol.

Billy Tubs and Larry spent some time in the shower that evening, but their efforts were not sufficient and both showed mud and poop on their faces and necks at breakfast in the morning. But manager Bud and his wife seldom paid attention to that sort of thing. Bud, himself didn't clean up much either.

And that was that, for our first bull riding. I figured it would be a long time before I loaded myself onto another bull.

## LOOKING FOR STRAYS AND BURDOCK

As I mentioned previously, the temporary summer manager at the Whit-more, Bud, was a negatory, lazy sort of fellow. He'd been raised on a ranch in Wyoming, but one way or the other he mentioned that his family had lost ownership of the ranch. If he'd been raised with the work habits he displayed when I knew him, I wasn't surprised that they had lost their place.

The only good thing I could see in him was he did have one fine horse. - that was the main thing. The other thing was he never let anybody but himself ride the animal and he took good care of that beautiful gelding.

We had a couple of wet days where we couldn't do any haying for a number of reasons, so Peck had stopped by and told me that I should go with Bud and search in the foothills for some missing steers that Peck hoped we could find alive. He said he was hoping they would not turn up as a pile of bones. And while we were looking through the brushy areas we should also chop all the Burdock and Canadian Thistle we saw. For that, we would need long-handled shovels, so we wouldn't need to dismount for every weed we chopped, and we should sharpen the shovels well before we started out. Out of earshot of the others, Peck told me that he didn't want Bud on that job alone, because Bud would likely just sit or lie someplace out of sight to smoke and snooze. Again I wondered why Peck didn't get rid of Bud. His tolerance for that indolent fellow was out of character, it seemed to me.

The ranch kept a few books on plants and diseases handy, which were seldom touched, so I borrowed one and read up on burdock, Latin name: *Arctium*. It turns out that the plant originated in the old world and likely got to North America hitchhiking in the hair of imported stock animals. Burdock spread wide and fast. Today we'd call it an invasive plant species but there was already plenty of it all over the Whitmore place.

It seems there are some useful medical applications of Burdock, but the negative side is that the sticky burs cause hair to wad up in the tails, manes, and ears of horses and other stock animals. When the weed is ripe, the burrs contain hundreds of tiny hooked slivers. That was nature's way of the plant spreading so successfully. If the slivers get around the animals' eyes, they cause irritation which leads to infection and at worst, can result in blindness. The affected eyes often resemble pink-eye and result in the need for doctoring which would not be necessary if not for the weedy plant. So the less Burdock you have in your pastures, the better off you and your stock will be.

Canadian Thistle (*Cirsium arvense*) is a perennial, noxious, broad-leafed weed that sends its roots deep - up to twenty feet down and spreads broadly - up to fifteen feet or more from the main stalk. What a nightmare that is! Like Burdock, Canadian Thistle came to North America from Eurasia and has some medicinal purposes. When used for pain relief and wound poultices it is sometimes referred to as Yarrow, "bloodwort" or "soldier's woundwort". This plant is a food source for some wild game, but most domestic stocks do not normally eat it. In some cases, it was reported to result in poor-tasting milk in cows that grazed on it.

Me on Babe and Bud on his fine gelding ready for a day of
Burdock chopping.

So in the case of both Burdock and Canadian Thistle, the less of either on the place the better off the stock and stockmen would be.

The battle with these weeds was ongoing and had already been waged for decades.

The plus side to the weed war was that I got to spend more time in the saddle and that suited me just fine.

So we spent the next several days riding through the foothills, chopping weeds, and hunting strays. We found five live steers which were in great shape and only one carcass which had been scavenged down to bare bones. We had no idea what killed it, but due to the broken long bones, a bear most likely bit through the dense bone to get at the marrow. But maybe that steer just died from old age and the ravages of the past winter. A critter destined to be raised for only two years, then be slaughtered for beef and burger might long for an existence like that of the dead one we found.

But we found plenty of Burdock and Canadian Thistle. It was easy to ride up next to a plant, lean over, and chop it off near the ground with the sharp shovel and that activity occupied most of our time all day long. I'm sure I must have chopped hundreds - maybe more than a thousand, of those weeds every day. I was glad we didn't have to gather up and dispose of the cut plants. Even with leather gloves on, I was beginning to get a callus in a new location on my right hand from gripping and thrusting the shovel.

Bud was one of those guys who liked to try to sound intelligent and smarter than he was. He'd criticize anybody who wasn't close enough to hear, even Peck, but never to their face. He told me this weed chopping was a waste of time because the weed would just sprout up again next spring, anyway. From what I had read, that was partly true, but in the meantime, if we chopped them, the sticky buds wouldn't be causing problems for the rest of the season, which was a most critical time of the year. And the main bunch of cattle wouldn't be in those fields until late the next fall. It was fall and winter when the cattle were most susceptible to eye irritation from the buds. So, I figured chopping the weeds was worthwhile.

The more I saw and listened to Bud, the more I wondered how he ever rated high enough for the job he currently held. He was a misfit and a forever malcontent, who produced nothing but bad vibrations.

And, not surprisingly, Bud was badly scared of snakes of any kind. When we'd come across a rattler, I would get off the horse, drop the reins and kill the snake with the shovel. Then I would cut the buttons off and stick them in my shirt pocket. I might figure out some use for them sometime, but never again for a necklace for a pretty girl. I saved the skins on some of the bigger serpents - just in case I found a use for them sometime in the future. I could skin a snake appropriately in less than five minutes.

Trying to sound like a wise, thoughtful old sage, Bud would mention how awful it would be if a buzz tail nailed me when I was afoot. Or how much I'd wished I had left the snake alone if my horse took off and I had to use Shank's mare (meaning my own legs) to get back to the ranch. My uncle had broken all the horses on the ranch, except Bud's, and the saddle mounts were trained to stand still if their rider dismounted and dropped the reins on the ground in front of the horse and they usually did that, so I wasn't worried. Yeah, the horse might run, but that was highly unlikely. I got the inkling that Bud would be pleased if I did get bit.

I ignored most of what Bud told me. I figured he just didn't want to be outdone or showed up on any issue, but he ran his mouth a lot, confirming his stupidity. One might say, he'd open his mouth and let his brains run out. But I was always careful with vipers anyway. I didn't want to give Bud the satisfaction of saying "I told you so." He'd gloat forever if I got bit.

We stopped for lunch one day near a small, clear creek. I was riding Babe, one of my favorite mares and she was one of the colts out of Goldy. I took the hackamore bridle off and let her graze on the fresh grass as we grazed on our sandwiches. Hackamores do not include a metal bit in the horse's mouth, which is kind to the horse and allows them to eat comfortably. I carried a set of rope hobbles, but never used them on most of the horses I rode as their use was not necessary.

Bud was going to stretch this lunch break to a full hour, or longer if he could. He laid back on the grassy bank as I wolfed down my sandwich and began poking around the side of the stream, cutting weeds as

I found them. There, right inside a fresh mule deer track was a nearly perfect arrowhead! I pocketed the flint projectile point and looked for more. I found no small chips of flint, which might indicate that some Indian had sat in that spot making arrow points, so I figured this point must have come from a single arrow, shot by some Indian hunter long ago as he hunted deer or buffalo. Random luck led me to it. Open eyes had revealed it to me.

A young Mule deer buck sailed out of the brush

In addition to the occasional deer, we encountered a couple of striped skunks *(Mephitis mephitis)* and a lone badger(*Taxidea taxus*), but most of our days were just spent chopping weeds with our shovels and me ignoring Bud and his neverending ridiculous palaver.

A couple of the short-time ranch hands, most of whom were scavengers had quit and Bud complained of some ailment which was an excuse for him to do as little as possible, making us three men short. There was still some hay in a big field to be cut, so I got assigned the job, but I was to use the "Big M' tractor with a seven-foot cutter bar, instead of a horse-drawn mower. I didn't care for the tractor, but it was work that needed to be done, so I did it.

The tractor was not nearly as interesting as driving a team of horses.

After a couple of days, Peck came with two newly hired men and I got off the tractor and went back up to my small log cabin at the main headquarters on the Little Hound Creek, and back to manufacturing hay with the two rake teams.

## NEW OWNER

The summer rocked along pretty much as the previous two had until one day in July when the ranch accountant came from Great Falls with the new owner of the Staunton Ranch Company. It was a horrible shock to us all. Peck and Stan had no idea the ranch company was even up for sale. The word was, old Staunton had a son, but he was worthless and killed himself on his motorcycle. He had one child, a teenage girl who had inherited the ranch and decided she wanted a big wad of money for who knows what? She, a city girl, had inherited a paradise but didn't see it the way I did. In fact, she had never even been there for more than an hour or two. The new owner, a young man with a lot of inherited money, (and whose name I won't even allude to here, but he was the heir and majority stockholder of a major gun manufacturing company) announced to all that there was going to be major changes in the operation, none of which sounded appealing to me. The ranch was to be modernized, meaning that most of the workhorses would be sold or taken to the slaughterhouse for dog food, I imagined. We were told that by the coming summer, the hay would be harvested with a new machine called a swather. No longer would hay be stacked with the overshot stacker. No longer would two men arrange the loose hay with pitchforks. No longer would the sixteen teams of workhorses have to be kept ready to go. The haying crew would be smaller and everything would be more efficient - like most other ranches all over the West had already become. The romance would be dead and gone.

By the standards of the 1950s, the Staunton Ranch Company managed by Peck, with Stan as foreman, was probably somewhere around at least thirty years behind the times in technology and mechanical equipment, but it made a good profit and provided a wonderful lifestyle. That lifestyle was soon to disappear.

One morning the new owner told me to load up those ugly old horses - Steamboat and Sally, Prince, and Hekate, even Big Sandy and Alice - the draft horses at Hound Creek - and get ready to truck them to Miles City. I knew they would be sold, and many of them would be slaughtered there, to wind up in a can of pet food. My Arizona Chauffeur's license put me in a position to drive the big truck with those old horses to their final corral.

That same morning my Mom called to tell me that I had been offered a scholarship to the University of Arizona. The total amount was five hundred and fifty dollars. If I made good - good grades that meant - the scholarship would be equaled for a second year. The estimated bare-bones cost of a year at that institution was around a thousand dollars. In the last three years, I had saved up over one thousand dollars, so as I drove the horses toward Miles City, intermittently in tears that I made sure no one saw, I decided to give college a go. I figured that if I could learn something that would give me independence from changes like I was about to witness at the ranch, I'd better do it. I'd no doubt have to leave the ranch to find a way to earn enough money to have a ranch of our own, anyway, so I was resolved to head for college.

I wanted more control of my own life. I wanted the worst tailender I would ever have to deal with, to be me, myself.

The Staunton Ranch Company with its twenty-two thousand acres, all the stock, buildings, and equipment sold for about about a quarter of a million dollars. If there was any way I could have done it, I would have mortgaged my very soul to hang onto it for Stan and me .... and our future families. It was a heartbreaking time for everyone who loved the place.

We never slacked off on our work, but nobody's heart was really in it after the announcement of the sale and the forthcoming changes. Meeting and listening to the new owner was really a downer for everyone. He had no practical knowledge or experience in ranching. I spent more overnight time at Boone's cabin in Squaw Hollow than ever before. Even that was a squatter situation, as Boone never owned the land and was apt to be ejected any time the new owner chose to do so. I didn't sleep so well the rest of the summer and noticed that Stan and Peck seemed worn down and depressed by the whole situation. Nobody liked the new owner or his plans. We were all mourning over the loss of the ranch and the lifestyle it offered. Our remorse was akin to the death of a loved family member.

A modern combine was contracted to harvest the oats.

In August we were told that the thrashing machine would no longer be used because the new owner had arranged to have a combine come the next week, which would save a lot of manpower, and therefore wages, and be more efficient. I figured the owner was making these great decisions from his big, fancy desk somewhere in a big smoggy city.

So, yet another part of the vanishing ranching life that I had come to love, would disappear.

# NORTHERN LIGHTS, DEVIL WARTS, AND BOONE'S MAGIC

## SUM BITCH STEW

Due to different combinations of circumstances, the most influential of which was the impending sale of the ranch, I wound up with several Sundays off - but, to my relief, with full payment of five bucks for the day. Now I had to think about saving what I could to pay for college. This summer, the new owner decided that no one was necessary at Elk Horn all summer. That made no sense, as they paid Boone next to nothing, but the young new owner was sure that he knew better. So Boone spent most of his time in his shack in Squaw Hollow. When Boone was at his cabin, I would ride up to spend time, often the whole evening, and overnight with him. He had no telephone or radio, but no advance notice to him was ever needed. He was always ready with a hearty welcome, a jug of whiskey, and plenty of new or re-told stories. I slept on the floor with a dried elk skin as a mattress.

Boone always had plenty of good stuff to eat. Sometimes, hunting season being open or not, he had a chunk of fresh deer or elk hanging in his meat house. He'd grown up taking wild meat as he needed and had never given up the practice. He also kept a supply of dried meat handy and often had a sack of some of it cut into little pieces to make it easier for him to chew or gum with his less-than-full set of grinder teeth. A bag of diced-up jerky mixed with some raisins, little bits of fat, maybe even some peanuts, small pieces of candy, or just plain sugar, tasted pretty good when a guy was hungry. And at eighteen years of age, and working long hours, I was nearly always hungry.

On his pot belly wood stove, he kept an extra large cast-iron Dutch oven full of what he called "Son of a Bitch Stew". The first time he mentioned it, I asked him which son of a bitch he had in there, all cut and cooked up and ready to chew on. And who could possibly taste good enough to eat, much less, swallow, anyway? And how would a feller go about cleaning a real son of a bitch, in the first place?

"Naw, naw, sprout. Ya don't unnerstan'. It's the kettle that's the son of a bitch. When it gets low, I just chunk some more of whatever's handy into that sum bitch. Sometimes it's taters, always some sort of meat, bacon, chunks of tallow, cut-up kidneys, heart, a cut-up groundhog, and now and then a fish from the creek, corn, carrots, turnips, rice, beans, leftover hot cakes, - whatever I can get a hold of. Then I toss in some salt, plenty of black pepper, a couple of spoons of ground cayenne, and a few squirts of Tabasco or steak sauce if I got some, and let 'er simmer. One time I was a tad tipsy and accidentally spilled almost half of a quart of whiskey into the thing. That batch was probably the best stew I ever tasted," he explained.

After that story, I figured almost any accident can be the mother of invention.

"Why, the stew jest sits there a'cookin and aging as I eat off'n it and keep adding to it. Sometimes it will last a month or more that way. Fact is, I reckon it could go on forever, like sourdough, and sometimes it nearly does, 'specially in the winter time," he declared. It sounded good to me and always tasted just fine. Everything was tender - and usually tasted about the same. In later years I discovered home-sized crock pots. When I think about it, I guess old Boone must have invented the crock pot!

Whatever he had to offer, after a snort or two of his bitter-tasting tax-free whiskey, a spoonful out of the sumbitch always tasted great. And I never got the trots or a belly ache from Boone's cooking. That old man had plenty of magic about him, of that I was certain.

## THE WHISKEY REBELLION

I asked Boone about how he got that untaxed whiskey. He studied me with squinted eyes for a few moments and then launched into a history lesson. I realized I was seeing ranching history disappear before my eyes at the time, but I was all eager ears for Boone's historical reflections.

"Back just after the Revolution, while George Washington was still president, the Treasury Department, headed by Alexander Hamilton - a bit of a nasty fellow - put a levy - that's a fancified word for a tax - on all whiskey made in this country," he said.

"No people ever like to be taxed and farmers who had stills set up to make extry cash from 'em were especially provoked by this action. So a bunch of them farmers got together one night and attacked and burned the house of the nearest federal government tax collector.

The whiskey makers got a big group together and Hamilton figured they threatened the survival of the new government, so he wanted to send in the army to put them down, but George Washington figured he could smooth talk the rebels into paying up. However that didn't work so Hamilton got Light Horse Harry Lee - who was General Robert E. Lee's daddy - and they took a force of several hundred, maybe thousands, of troops up to Pennsylvania to enforce the whiskey tax," Boone explained.

When they saw how serious the government was about collecting the tax, the whiskey rebels scattered, all except a couple who were caught and convicted of treason, and set to be hanged, but they were later excused, 'stead of executed, by President George Washington.

This whole mess upset Thomas Jefferson, who already had a hefty dose of dislike for Hamilton and the other Federalists trying to influence the new government. Jefferson thought using military force on American citizens was a bad idea. However the tax on whiskey remained and it was used to pay for government mistakes, expenses, and excesses, and still is, 'til this very day.

Me on Bing ready to go to Boone's cabin. The spring house is on the left.
Pooche's summer house, just outside Peck and Vera's back door,
is seen on the right.

But whiskey is still being homemade and if a feller is cagey and careful he can avoid paying the dag-gone tax or getting hisself hung for dodging it," he told me.

The way Boone wove history together, including the names of so many well-known forebears, was fascinating to me. If our school history teachers had done it that way, we might all have become professors of history. Grover Boone Austin had a lot of natural talents. The old man was truly inspirational to me.

## DEVIL WARTS

The first summer I knew Boone, 1958, I had warts on the ends of my thumbs and other places on my fingers. Those unwanted digital hitchhikers were painful every time I bumped one or touched anything. Boone saw me wince one time and grabbed my hand in his gnarled clutch, looked it over, and told me he had a cure for "them devil warts", as he called them. He told me to have Vera get me a little bottle of olive oil from the drugstore next time she was in town and then I should cut a small piece of Willow twig, carry it right inside the oil bottle and daub the oil on my warts as many times a day as I could.

162

"Fifty, sixty times a day, if you can," he urged. With that bottle in a front shirt pocket, you should remember to use it each time you take a sip of water or pee - and lots of times in between.

"The more you oil them warts, the sooner they will wither up their roots and leave you. Devil warts don't like olive oil," he said.

On Monday I asked Vera at breakfast if next time she was in town, she could pick me up the smallest bottle of olive oil she could find because I was going to carry it in my pocket and daub my finger warts.

"Olive oil, - warts! You've been talking to old Boone. He's nothing but an old wart himself," she declared.

Before I left the table, Vera set a two-ounce bottle of oil in front of me. So, she'd used Boone's cure, too, it seemed, but she'd never give him any credit.

Well, after about ten days of daubing the warts dozens of times every day, all those troublesome warts just disappeared. I got so I could use the oil without stopping or even slowing the rake team. From then and into my adult life I have passed that handy cure on to many other people, most of whom reported success with ridding themselves of painful thumb and fingertip warts. The ones for whom the cure failed probably did not daub their warts often enough, I figure.

So Boone's magic is still working. It's a legacy of sorts, I reckon.

Usually, I took a slab of bacon or side meat (which is uncured bacon) - and I mean a slab - not just a pound of thinly sliced strips like grocery stores commonly sell nowadays - I mean a hunk of hog side meat of at least four to six pounds. Or I'd take something else nice that I got from the Hound Creek cook to supplement Boone's larder. Once in a while, she'd send a whole fresh pie, but a bag of cookies or sweet biscuits was nearly always available.

Boone liked eating groundhogs, too. They went well in the sum bitch stew. So I'd take the 22 rifle along and try to pop one or two on the way up to his place. There seemed to be no end to whistle pigs around Little Hound Creek, especially in the rocky areas near the headquarters. I was careful to stick the right front foot of each one into my pocket for the fifty cents bounty from Peck. My skill in disarticulating a foot joint had improved to where I could do it in less than thirty seconds without breaking any of the bones. Boone would have me skin the critters, then gut and wash them off real carefully in the creek before I cut them up to put in the big pot. Most everything that came out of the Sum Bitch kettle tasted the same. It was just like a modern Crock Pot, in that regard.

## NORTHERN LIGHTS

One evening in August Boone got to telling stories about his favorite subject - which was killin' old time "Indins". He was telling of their superstitions and their magic, or medicine, as they called it. However much he seemed to hate them, he revered their bush skills and respected their magic - the old-time Indians, that is, not the modern ones like those we shanghaied out of the Great Falls bars, for whom Boone told me, the only magic came in a bottle of white man's fire water. Those Indins were just a step above the drifters hired as haying crew - they were just scavengers.

He talked about "Indins" skills at reading "sign", by which he meant tracks and other evidence (such as poop, bent grass, and broken bush branches) of the passage of animals, whether they be the two-legged or the four-legged kind. Most of the Indians of the better-known, aggressive tribes of the region, like the Blackfeet, Sioux, and Crow were pretty good at figuring out signs, but he assured me that he and his brothers were way better. He added that he knew of other old-time white men who could read sign as good or better'n any band of Indins. He said because the red-hide savages so far outnumbered the whites back then, the whites that survived had to be better at tracking and leaving false sign to throw pursuers off, than their red-hide enemies, or they would have all been rubbed out, right away - and America would be left with nothing but a bunch of howling, murderous gangs of wild savages.

Boone told me that all "Indins" paid close attention to abnormalities like the extremely rare white buffalo, or the seldom-seen albino critter of any species, as well as people and animals that acted different - or even crazy in the case of humans. Some of the "medicine men" were clearly crazy in some form, but they were shown extra respect by their kinsmen in the tribe and those different folks carried a lot of influence. That sounded like modern politicians today.

Celestial events were some of the major concerns for all Indins. Full or even partial eclipses of the sun or moon would cause the savages to set up sweat lodges right away to cleanse their souls - trying to make it right with their Gods. They'd do lots of dances and carry on for extended spells as they attempted to pacify their God, or as they referred to Him .. the Great Spirit, or whatever their tribe called him. The Sioux called him Wakantanka. Some of the Canadian Indians believed in a celestial power figure they called Gitche Manitou.

Boone told me that a lot of white folks and Indians disdained the Pawnee tribe for being scared of whites, but he said he and a companion ran into some wild ones that scared the daylights out of him until he got 'em all three shot and scalped. That happened in what is now southeastern Montana or maybe it was clear over in South Dakota. The state lines weren't set up yet. He and a partner had been hunting buffalo on the Little Missouri River (that was the main drainage directly east of the Yellowstone River) and they got interested in reports of gold being picked up out of some small creeks, so they headed east for a few days but found only trouble and none of the yellow metal.

Boone was as spooky about Northern Lights as every Indian was. He said some of what the 'indins' believed made sense to him. He paid attention to their beliefs, just in case they might be at least partly right.

Some tribes believed that the lights foretold war, disease, and famine. Others figured the ghosts of their slain enemies were trying to come back to life to take their revenge. Those without scalps never got a chance to come back, therefore every dead enemy should be scalped, he told me. He said he and his family always scalped dead Indians as a way of assuring that they would not have to fight them again. After several whiskeys, he told me that it was hard for him to resist scalping Indians that died of natural causes. Why, he might even lift the hair from some of them that worked on the ranch, if the chance came his way! I was convinced he meant that and I was glad he didn't mention my friend, Broken-Nosed Joe.

Boone told me that the Mandans of North Dakota saw the northern lights as coming from fires over which their enemies' medicine men and warriors cooked their dead victims in big kettles. I wondered if that meant they were cannibals. A guy probably couldn't tell if they were put in the sumbitch stew.

At any rate, Boone told me, the weird lights were nothing to fool around with or be casual about. A feller should never whistle at the lights, but if they were getting too close, clapping your hands might get them to back off. For sure they were "big medicine", and represented grave danger of the most evil kind imaginable.

As I sat spellbound by Boone's tales, one evening I realized that his homemade wooden chairs - which were complete strangers to cushions - I had never felt uncomfortable to my backside, even after sitting for several hours. Maybe it was due to the intensity of my interest in his stories. I suppose the whisky played a part, too.

One Sunday night after being regaled for hours as we sipped Boone's whiskey, I checked my Timex wristwatch and figured I'd better head for the ranch as Stan had mentioned a special project for extra early the next morning.

It was almost midnight when I threw the blanket and saddle back on Reuben, one of the outfit's best saddle horses and he was one of the gelded sons of old Goldie.

We had at least an hour to travel home, maybe more as it was pure dark that clear, chilly, windless, moonless night. A good walk was all I could demand of the horse over that irregular, rock-strewn trail along the creek, especially in my tipsy condition.

As I climbed aboard Reuben, Boone offered me a pinch of his Copenhagen. I took a small pinch just to humor him, then spit it out when I was out of sight. Copenhagen always made me dizzy, especially after the priming I got from the corn squeezin's.

About fifteen minutes from Boone's cabin I was drowsy and half asleep when Reuben suddenly snorted and stopped up so short. I lurched forward and felt the saddle horn in my belly. I opened my eyes to see dancing lights overhead. Pastels of avocado green and faded red were undulating in the northern sky. Reuben was not a twitchy horse but he went stiff, backed up a couple of steps, and snorted again.

There was no wind, but I thought I heard faint, weird, high-pitched noises, like a bunch of women wailing. Reuben snorted again. I was fully awake and getting ready to be really spooked myself.

Reuben inhaled and snorted again - big time as he tossed his head. I thought I heard a sound in the bushes. Maybe a bear? I pulled the .22 from its scabbard and wished I had the 30/40 Krag.

The lights slowly morphed, and lazied around, like smoke does when there's no steady breeze. The lights seemed eerily sullen and purely malevolent in their slow movements. Clearly, this was the evil witches' business.

The horse and I were transfixed for what seemed like half of forever, but it was probably only two or three minutes before the lights seemed to reluctantly fade away and move off to the east.

It was strange, ominous magic for sure, and it was the first time I had ever seen the Aurora Borealis.

As I nudged Reuben with my heels he hesitated, then with a second light kick of my heels, he went into a slow walk, headed toward home. The gelding kept looking to his right and left as we slowly went along the trail.

My attention was divided between the disappearing lights and the thick willow brush bordering the creek that might be concealing a bear. The horse seemed to be paying no attention to the brush, so I figured there must be no bruin or other terrestrial bugger nearby. I'd never heard any stories of men being attacked by bears in recent times, anyway.

This was the first time I'd ever seen the lights and probably the first time for Reuben, too. I was sure glad Boone had told me about them. It would be several years before I saw them again - that happened in 1967 - eight years later - in northwest Arctic Alaska on the Kobuk River.

My Timex wristwatch read two o'clock in the morning when I put Ruben in his stall and rubbed him down. I gave him a treat of grain and told him what a good horse he truly was. I opened the door to my cabin at two thirty and fell into my bed.

Boone's whiskey and his incessant stories comforted me some, though. He was eighty-nine or maybe older than ninety (he said he wasn't sure) years old by 1960 and his tales of Montana back in the eighteen hundreds were more interesting to me than any movie had ever seen, except maybe "The Big Sky".

Boone told me that at first he and the rest of his family didn't really hate "Indins", they just steered clear of them all, until some Blackfeet got Mike. They'd heard about Custer and his whole cavalry brigade - or at least two hundred and ten men - getting all rubbed out, scalped, and mutilated by Sioux and Cheyenne in late June 1876, and the Austins figured it was best to stay away from all "Indins", as it was sometimes difficult to tell one tribe from another. Boone said he was "a little feller" just about six years old then. The Austin family made no trouble for any of the red skins. They pretty much thought of them in a category similar to that of grizzly bears - a dangerous breed apart and best left alone, unless you just had to deal with them.

He said that he was the youngest of the boys in the family (which reminded me that being the only one, I was both the youngest and oldest boy in my immediate family - I could call it either way, which might be handy to know some time) and from an early age Boone had accompanied his Pa and older brothers on hunting and trapping trips all over the Montana territory. His mother and the little kids which were all girls stayed in the stout little log house they had built near the bank over on the Smith River. She kept a garden, caught fish, occasionally shot a deer or elk, lots of Prairie Chickens and Fool's Hens, and maintained the family headquarters for sometimes a month or more between visits from the menfolk. Boone never mentioned her complaining - that was just the way of life for women on the American western frontier in those days. It was, however, uncommonly lucky she and her kids were never molested nor "done in" by wild "Indins".

They hunted buffalo in the Judith Basin while there were still isolated herds of up to a few hundred animals, but they watched the numbers drop every year until they finally gave up on that country and moved westerly where there was always plenty of elk. He said the elk were thinning out in the open country, too, but they were plentiful and easily taken in the mountains and timbered areas. The family particularly liked the Little Belt Mountains.

They shot wild game mostly to sell to miners and town people. In hard times they would shoot deer or antelope, but they concentrated their efforts on the bigger critters as they had so much more meat for the amount of lead and powder spent and the meat was what brought them money. They shot a lot but did not waste ammunition. The family was trained to "aim small" with their iron-sighted weapons.

He told me that some folks had persnickety likes and dislikes. Some people wanted bear meat - it's always tender - so they pretty much shot every bear they could get to. "Course some bears were bad stinkers and had to be left where they fell. In cold times they saved the hides to sell as well. They encountered only a few grizzlies (*Ursus arctos or Ursus horribilis*). Most of the bears they killed were black bears (*Ursus americanus*).

When ranchers got to worrying about wolves getting their cattle, the Austin boys went to spending a lot of time being wolfers. Any wolf sighted in the open country was run down by the mounted hunters and most did not escape being shot. A good horse could allow a man to easily kill a wolf. Some of the ranchers paid a decent bounty of wolves of any age or size. Boone helped smoke wolves out of their dens, as pups brought the same bounty as an adult and were easy pickings, he told me.

As the game became more scarce, the Austin brothers split up for weeks at a time, usually, two or sometimes three of the brothers together with a string of pack horses set off for indeterminate periods of time. Seldom would they go off alone. Occasionally a friend from outside the immediate family would join in on a trip.

To preserve meat for longer periods of time they would smoke the quarters until a distinct crust appeared which would dry and keep the meat fine without spoiling and free of fly blo for sometimes a week or longer in the hottest weather. At every overnight stop, they would hang the quarters and make a fire. Sometimes in warm weather, they made a fire underneath to keep flies away. Rain and damp weather were bad and sometimes caused meat to spoil real fast.

Late one fall in November or so, his oldest brother, Mike, struck off for the Little Blackfoot River area over towards Helena to check out a rumor that two large packs of wolves were raising Cain with a rancher's stock over that way.

When Mike, whom I surmised was in his late teens or early twenties, didn't show up back at the cabin for a long spell, Boone and another brother headed up the Missouri River, then to the Little Blackfoot to look for him. Boone said that right off they found way too much "Indin" sign to be comfortable and were worried about Mike. As they were only two very young men, they were careful, made no fires, and traveled mostly at night. They knew about where Mike planned to be, but it took more than a week to find his camp and what they found - Boone said, - well, it was awful to see then and to think about ever since.

He said the Blackfeet had killed and mutilated his favorite brother, Mike. Mike's body was stuck full of arrows, his eyes were gouged out, he had been scalped, and other body parts, including his whanger (penis), were cut off. It looked to Boone and his brother like Mike had been alive while some of the mutilations were being done to him. In fact, they were sure of that. Boone said he and his brother built a fire right there and burned Mike's tortured remains and decided to go on the warpath themselves.

The bloody Indians had never been hurt or bothered by any members of the Austin family, but then they'd gone and done this to poor Mike. There was no call for them to do that. Naturally, anybody in a situation like this would take it very personal -and the Austins sure did.

So Boone and his remaining two brothers took every opportunity to kill any and all Indians of any type that they could find. After leaving the site of Mike's mutilation, further up the Little Blackfoot drainage, they found a small camp with two teepees. The young Austin wolvers set up on both sides of the teepees and started killing just as the sun was coming up. Boone shot the first male that came out, then he and his brother shot two more bucks with their rifles. They rushed right into the camp and killed a couple of squaws and two kids, using their hand axes. That was the first seven red hides they sent directly to the devil, he told me.

"We scalped 'em all, too," he assured me. That way they'd have no chance of causing us any trouble in the future, he proclaimed.

For the next several years anytime they would even smell an "Indin", they would break off their market hunting and go after the savages. Boone told me they got so they could sniff out an Indin from miles away. Then, finally, they didn't run across any more loose "Indins" in the country. He said he wished they'd got 'em all, but they hadn't been that lucky. So now everybody in the country had to put up with those that survived the Austin brothers' crusade. Now those savage buggers had special reservations and extra privileges and protection and everything, including welfare.

He claimed they killed over thirty-six red hide "Indins", but after an evening of drinking, I noticed the number sometimes grew to well over three hundred. I guessed that the final count didn't really matter much, except maybe to the Indians. Late one night, after a couple of Boone's whiskeys, I mentioned that maybe we should hang and scalp the new owner of the ranch. Boone said he "jest might danged well do that". I doubt that I would have tried to stop him, but the opportunity never came up.

Boone said that as the country got all "claimed and fenced up" and then, even more, fenced in by ranchers, miners, preachers, schoolteachers, homesteaders, and the like, he decided he'd have to go to cowboying to make a living. It wasn't nearly as interesting as living had been before too many people showed up in the territory, but it sure was better than hanging around any town, doing nothing but smoking and drinking rot gut whiskey and looking at the painted ladies.

Boone at his squatter's cabin, bringing out a pan of wash water to toss.

I never heard Boone mention having a long-term woman or begetting any kids. I don't recall him ever mentioning chasing any woman or feeling especially lusty toward any, either.

As for the future, Boone told me he figured he'd just stay at Squaw Hollow, maybe get a job tending cows for somebody, but things sure had gone to the devil as far as he was concerned and it was all getting lots worse - and fast. "Jest too many fancy people nowadays, all awantin' ever thing to be clean, easy, and packaged ready for 'em, but not wanting or knowing how to do a blamed thing for themselves, 'cept complainin'" he lamented.

"Why, sometimes I think we were better off when the "Indins" held the territory. At least we could shoot those savages that bothered us, and even have satisfaction and be praised for doing it," he concluded.

The last I heard about Boone came from Peck in 1967, when I stopped by to pick up my Grandma to take with me to Alaska and to visit Peck, Vera, and Stan on my way north. Peck told me that Boone was driving a stock truck full of horses and went off the road into the Missouri River and he drowned, along with all the horses. He would have been about ninety-seven years old, or maybe older. Some people suggested that he might have been drinking too much of his cheap whiskey.

## THE SAD, INEVITABLE ENDING

The days grew longer for me, somehow. Maybe it was my feeling of witnessing the end of an era and a way of life. The term tsunami was not in common use back then, but the avalanche was, and that word adequately described the rush of negative emotions that repeatedly swept me out of my usual positive mental state and dropped me into a dark emotional abyss. The life I longed for was going to disappear right before my eyes before I could even savor it for very long. The horses I loved, but never owned - most were going to be sold and many would be killed to feed some city person's kitty cat, and replaced with machinery. Man, did I ever feel blue ... no, I felt far worse. I felt rotten, betrayed, forsaken, sick, and lonesome.

With the University of Arizona cranking up in August, I had to depart before most of the fall cattle drives took place, but we did take a bunch of culls and older steers down from Elkhorn all the way to Cascade. Stan and I with the two dogs made the drive without any trouble. I was trying to consciously soak up everything I could about the experience so that somehow, it would stay with me. I knew that I needed these memories to last a lifetime. I could visit ranches to reacquaint myself with the smells of grass, cattle, and horses, but more real memories of my own activities of that sort, would not be in the making.

One afternoon as we were sitting by a clear, cold stream, my Uncle Stan asked me what was wrong. I think he already knew and was feeling about the same, as I was.

"I'm just feeling miserable that this will be the last time we do this sort of thing together. Pushing these cattle up the ramp to the rail cars in Cascade will be to me, like walking up the stairs to a hangman's noose or into exile. There goes the best part of my life, off to the slaughterhouse," I told him.

"Well, like everything else in life, you know good things just about have to come to an end sometime, so enjoy 'em while you got 'em", and then keep your eyes wide open for new ones. Life really is good, if you work at making it that way," he counseled.

After about six days of slow trailing to minimize shrink we spent the last night at the old Loy Place, close to the Missouri River at Cascade. The house smelled musty and very old, as always. It reminded me of the smells in my Great Grandma Hollander's house in Iowa. Her canned fruits and vegetables were delightful tasting, but her house smelled musty, like the old Loy Place. I welcomed this one last time to be there. I knew that I was going to be homesick for that place and all the others. Most of all, I was going to miss this simple, honest, old-fashioned lifestyle and the people that followed the old ways.

We hung around until mid-afternoon for the final short push of less than a mile to the railhead. We let the cattle fill up as much as they wanted to on good grass and water. As I watched them sucking up the water, I realized I had been spiritually sucking up as much of Montana cowboying as I could. Once in the stockyard, the buyers would want the cattle to stand overnight without access to water to drop their weight as much as possible before going onto the scales - a decent buyers shrink they called it - so there was no point in us putting the stock in the yard earlier than necessary.

As we started them across the bridge two of the three-year-old steers broke away from the bunch and without pausing, went over the bank and jumped into the Missouri River. It was like they knew the slaughterhouse awaited and were trying to escape. Lucky for the steers, for me, and for Goldie, the water level was lower than normal, making the current less fierce and exposing a few gravel bars near each bank of the river. The river was wide there, which also made the crossing easier.

I remembered what I had heard Stan say so often, - "When in doubt, let your horse do the thinking."

Stan hollered at me to do what I knew I had to do, which was to follow the steers. I think he saw it as an opportunity for me to play at real cowboy action, while I still could. I sure did see it that way.

As usual, I was riding Goldie, the big, wise, old mare with more cow sense than any other horse I had ever used. She had more smarts than most people I knew, too. And Goldie had foaled some of the best saddle horses on the ranch, including Reuben, Vic, and Babe.

Too bad that our politicians and the young girl heir to the Staunton Ranch Company didn't have half the common sense and smarts that fine old mare displayed.

When Goldie reached the bank, she hesitated momentarily, then turned and headed for a gentler slope to the water. The two steers were rolling in fat and I could see their heads and the top of their backs just above the water as they swam away. I gently stroked the big mare's flank with my spurs and she stepped in, then when the water was knee-deep she lunged forward. The river was deep in the channel right there and Goldie sensed it. Our heads never went underwater, but I was soaked almost up to my nipples. It was a warm day in August, but the water felt shockingly cold. I held onto my hat and loosened the reins to give Goldie full control of her head to swim after the steers as we all headed for the opposite bank. Goldie, with me on her back, arrived less than a minute behind the cattle.

The steers shook off the water, then stood in place. They seemed relieved and worn out from the swim. Goldie, after a quick shake to rid herself of most of the water, moved up right next to the pair of escapees, keeping an eye on those troublemakers. We all remained in place, catching our breath for a minute or so. Then Goldie got next to one steer and nudged it to move.

Soon we headed the two critters back uphill toward the road where they fell in place and joined up with the rest of the bunch.

Stan had held his horse back to keep the steers going in the right direction. I'm sure he took in all of the action. He gave me his curt, single nod of approval, and we continued down the highway to the rail yard corrals.

Not until twenty-eight years later, when I swam horses across rivers in Bolivia on several occasions, while spending a couple of months trying to set up a Jaguar hunting business in that country, would I again swim a horse across a river.

Swimming horses across a flooded river in central Bolivia in March of 1988.

Just before dark, we had them all in the stockyard. It was late in the day, so we'd timed it right. The buyers would get their shrink all right, but no more than was absolutely necessary.

I was beginning to feel downright chilly from the soaking I got in the river crossing. Dismounting and pouring the water out of my boots helped some.

I was glad that I got the chance to do this unexpected retrieval job, and I think Stan was too.

Peck and Vera had come down in the jeep and brought Stan and me a set of clean clothes to wear to dinner. That was especially lucky for me after my unscheduled dip in the river. We changed our duds over at Bill's garage, washed our faces, and slapped on some Old Spice after-shave lotion that Peck had put in our sack of clothes. I had clean socks but the inside of my boots soon had them wet and chilly.

The cattle buyers were waiting for us and took us and the brand inspector, who appeared to be as old as Boone - maybe even older - to the local restaurant for dinner. That brand inspector had the bushiest "geezer hairs" growing long from his eyebrows that I had ever seen. The cattle buyers had heard of the sale of the ranch and seemed to want to make this a big "grand finale" evening for everybody. And they weren't cheap about it. We all ate twenty-four-ounce Porterhouse steaks with salad and a baked potato, and for dessert, we had a big piece of apple pie with vanilla ice cream on top. Outside, just after dinner, a brand new bottle of Old Grand Dad was passed around for each man, including me, to take a long pull or two on.

Everyone's favorite libation.

As I was packing my stuff for the last time, I decided to keep the dandy batwing chaps, spurs, and a one-ear hackamore bridle that Stan had given to me. Just maybe I'd get an opportunity to use them sometime, someplace. I left most of my clothes, including the pointy-toed boots, the old leather jacket, and my well-worn hat for somebody else who might get some use out of them. The bunkhouse had a pile of stuff like that already, so I added to the pile .. and no doubt, the smell.

I felt lucky that I had been given the brief, but nevertheless a thorough taste of old-time cowboy life in Montana for the past three summers. But everything was laced with sadness that evening, especially for me, as I knew this was the end of my wonderful, but all too abbreviated, life as a cowboy. The tincture of time would spend a long spell trying to heal my heartache.

## FORMAL SCHOOLING

Before I headed up to Montana, and before I graduated from high school in 1960, my Mom had insisted that I apply for every scholarship available, even though I did not plan to attend college. But to satisfy her I sent out several applications. I really intended to stay right there on the ranch, but the horrible surprise events of the summer of 1960 meant that was no longer in the cards.

My grades were excellent, as were most of my teachers in my senior year. Mark O'Malley taught math and science. He made his students want to learn, and to really learn to think analytically, not just by memorizing stuff. He insisted that we be able to THINK, rationally. He reminded us that none could consider themselves to be educated until they had mastered "the calculus". When I did enter college at the University of Arizona, I took the exams for Algebra and Trigonometry and "maxed" both of them, giving me five college credits with a grade of "A" right off the bat, but I never did take "the calculus", so I remain uneducated to this day, I guess.

Having never been interested in grammar, and having only uninspiring English teachers, I initially wound up in "Bone head" English, to be taken for no credit, but my essay saved me from that ignominious placing and I was able to take regular English, for full credit. Without this reprieve, I could not have qualified for a Bachelor's degree in just over two years.

The University of Arizona in Tucson was only about an hour's drive from my folk's home, but I still had misgivings about enrolling in school, especially if my heart pump was not going to hold out well enough to give me a long, active life.

So the week before the college courses began, I visited a private cardiologist in Tucson to see if my ticker was good enough to justify the effort and expense of four or more years of college. If I wasn't going to live long, I'd just spend my savings on hunting, or even work for free on a cattle ranch - for the rest of my short life. I expected that most of my thousand dollars or so in savings would be used to pay the heart specialist. But oh well, I could always go back to mowing lawns if I needed to.

The kindly doctor gave me a thorough examination and told me that my murmur was barely discernible and that my four years of monthly Bicillin shots had not been necessary. He summarized by telling me that I had been the victim of a gross misdiagnosis, but my exercising, especially the running, had been well worthwhile. He then shook my hand, laid his hand on my shoulder, wished me the best of luck, and told me his services were "on the house". What a wonderful surprise! I would never forget that, and as a dentist, I tried to pay back his exemplary generosity with similar actions for numerous people that came my way. Whether for a free set of dentures or just a filling or an extraction, I told each patient that the gratis aspect must be kept just between me and the patient. I didn't want the word to get around. I did still have to make a living.

Being thoroughly humbled by that doctor, I decided that if the Baird Scholarship people, who didn't even know me, were going to gamble five hundred and fifty dollars per year on my schooling, I'd better try to treat them the same as I had everybody that I had worked for, although I'd actually be working mostly for myself this time. Working mostly for oneself is true when one is working for a regular employer, too, of course, but it's much more personal when it comes to schooling which is like your own business. I resolved to do the best job I could in school and to get out of school as soon as possible.

The wonderful news from the cardiologist took a couple of days to really soak in, then I realized that this was one of the most important gifts in life so far. It was another turning point in my life.

In fact, as my scholarship money was only for two years, I would aim at getting my Bachelor of Science degree in that amount of time, and get accepted to a good dental school. Schooling was going to be a full-time effort for me. I would just have to grit my teeth, stifle my urges, and do it! My resolve was firm and after two years and the summer in between, I had nearly all the requirements for a Bachelor of Science degree in Biology. During my second year in dental school, I took a night course in English literature at Portland State College which completed the requirements for a Bachelor of Science in Biology.

I graduated from the University of Oregon Dental School in May 1966, then completed a year of post-graduate dental studies at the Marine Hospital in Baltimore, before being transferred to the Indian Health Service in Alaska. In June 1969 I was honorably discharged and have been in Alaska ever since.

## MY UNCLE STAN NASON

After my departure, Stan and Peck stayed on to help with the ownership transition of the ranch company. It was a disappointing and frustrating time for them both. They loved the place and had devoted their lives to it, and it was painful seeing it sectioned, mutilated, horses sold to be ground into pet food, and key land parcels amputated by the new owner.

The new owner ordered a huge reduction in the number of horses, including the sale of all but two teams of draft horses.

Expensive, complicated new equipment was brought in, along with people to train ranch hands in the operation of the new gear. Stan and Peck figured too much training of ranch hands was a waste of time and money, as most hands were drifters and would probably not be around more than a couple of months or so, at most. It had always been that way. And that was not apt to change much, or soon.

The new owner decided to sell off large parts of the Staunton Ranch Company beginning with Squaw Hollow where Boone squatted in his old cabin. The Loy place near the Missouri River and the little town of Cascade was next to go on the block. The best all-around ranch of the lot, so far as operating on its own was concerned, was the Whitmore place, which was soon sold, and not long after that, the summer range at Elkhorn changed ownership.

Peck retired and my uncle quit and went to work for a ranch located a bit southeast of Great Falls, but that operation didn't live up to the standards he and Peck had maintained at Hound Creek, so, disappointed, Stan quit.

On a trip to visit his mother - that was Gram to me - Stan met a gal named Carole that proved to be just exactly the right one for him. He enrolled in the Ferrier School in Phoenix, Arizona, and became a full-time, licensed horseshoer. And he got married at about fifty years of age or so.

Beginning in 1970 Stan and I made several extended trips to Oregon, Montana, and Arizona to look at ranches. For the next twenty years, it was still our dream to have a place of our own. We figured Stan would live on the place and run it, along with his wife and son, Steve, who was born in 1975, but we never could find an affordable place that looked to me like it would do anything but work Stan to death. Feedlots and huge ranches owned by old ranching families with substantial financial resources had put most small ranch operations like we dreamed about, out of the realm of practicability for us. The ranching lifestyle we sought had become a thing of the past, or at least out of reach for us. If the Staunton Ranch Company had been available for a quarter of a million dollars ten years later than it sold, I would have moved heaven and earth, even mortgaged my soul, to acquire it. If I was able to get it, I doubt I would have ever come to Alaska.

For close to thirty-five years after leaving Montana Stan lived in southern Arizona, making his living as a full-time professional horseshoer. Once he lamented to me that he was just doing manicures on peoples' horse pets' toenails, instead of keeping real working horses on the job, but he was relieved to be independent of the financially over-indulged, self-important fellow that had bought and broken up the old

Staunton Ranch Company. He adapted well to the southern desert, but his heart was always in Montana.

My Uncle Stan was still alert mentally and active physically until he passed away in 2007. He somewhat forecast his coming demise by giving away the last of his horses. When I heard that he had done that, I figured he was expecting to be taking that long last ride soon.

I made a point of calling Stan about every week or so. He always thanked me for the call. And I took the family to visit with him and his family every other year. In 2007 I went down to Tucson to get a second opinion prior to my bilateral knee replacements, expecting to spend some time with Stan as well, but he passed away two days before I got there.

Carole made arrangements for Stan's cremation and we had a memorial for him out at the corrals he built near their home. Carole told me that she wanted his ashes to be scattered near our lodge at Trail Creek, one hundred sixty-five miles above the Arctic Circle. Stan and their son Steve had been there and both loved the place.

When I began scattering Stan's ashes, I decided to take some back to Hound Creek, as his heart was truly always there.

In June of 2008 my wife, Teresa, daughters Bess and Kate and I flew to Spokane, rented a motor home, and drove to Montana. We spent the first night on the beautiful Little Blackfoot River. In the morning we drove on to Hound Creek. I took a short cut which would put us at the Whitmore ranch, but things looked different after fifty years. A county road grader was stopped alongside the road, so I asked if we were on the right route to the Whitmore place. He said he didn't know of a ranch by that name. We drove on and saw a sign indicating the place was now called the Rumney Ranch.

We saw no Hereford cattle. They had been replaced by black Angus stock.

We crossed the same old steel bridge over Hound Creek and saw a young girl on a fine-looking horse picking up the mail. I asked her if anyone was at home and she said her mother was at the house, so we drove up and I asked the lady if we might scatter my uncle's ashes in the big hayfield. She asked the name of my uncle when I said Stan Nason, she knew who he was and told me it was fine to drive up to the field.

After we scattered the ashes in the light breeze I took the family toward a nearby swale in which used to sit an old horse-drawn mowing machine. Stan and I had taken parts off that machine to use on others. The rusty little mower was in the same place I had last seen it more than fifty years before.

A rattlesnake tuned up as we approached the mower. Our youngest daughter, Kate, hollered that she wanted the rattle, Bess screeched that she never thought she would see one in real life, and Teresa screamed for everyone to get away from the snake. I picked up a couple of rocks and as the snake made its way toward the mowing machine I hit it about six inches behind the head, partially disabling it. If it had gotten under the mower we might not have been able to safely get it.

We were wearing light shoes - Crocks mostly - so I told everyone to be very careful where they put their feet as the area was known to have lots of buzztails. Another rock from close range smashed the head of the serpent and I then beheaded the thing. It was large for that area at forty-eight inches in length with ten buttons in its rattle.

Back at the motor home I used scissors to cut down the center of the belly scales, peeled off the skin, and placed it on a piece of cardboard to dry flat. We decided to eat the meat for dinner, along with the steaks we had bought in Helena. Steak and snake make a good substitute for surf and turf in rural Montana.

We returned to the ranch house and I mentioned to the lady that my uncle and I had built the round corral in 1959 and asked if we might stay in our rented motorhome near the corral and creek for the night. She said it would be fine.

Our daughters, Bess and Kate were fishing for rainbows near the old corral when a pick-up came at high speed down the road. The driver lived in Peck and Vera's old house and was manager for the ranch's new owners. He was obviously angry at seeing the motor home when he jumped out of the vehicle. I walked up to him and told him I had permission to be there and why we had come. When he heard the name, Stan Nason, he mellowed out immediately.

As we visited I told him I'd like to take the kids up to Boone's old cabin. The man was shocked to hear that I had known Grover Boone Austin. He said that the old cabin had been designated a Montana historical building, but the gate was locked by the new owner, so we did not get to visit the old squatter's cabin.

The next day we drove up the road toward Elk Horn as far as the motor home would take us before going on to Great Falls.

We made a tour of Montana, starting with Charlie Russel's home and museum in Great Falls, then on to the Custer Battlefield near Hardin, before going to Yellowstone and several other interesting places in that part of the country.

I noticed the wonderful smells of Montana, but in no other place were they so strong and influential on me as at Hound Creek.

About 2006. Stan and me next to the pickup I bought for him in Tucson.